The Craftster Guide to
NIFTY, THRIFTY, and KITSCHY
CRAFTS

Fifty Fabulous Projects from the Fifties and Sixties

LEAH KRAMER

TEN SPEED PRESS
Berkeley | Toronto

Ten Speed Press
Box 7123
Berkeley, California 94707
www.tenspeed.com

Distributed in Australia by Simon and Schuster
Australia, in Canada by Ten Speed Press Canada,
in New Zealand by Southern Publishers Group, in
South Africa by Real Books, and in the United
Kingdom and Europe by Airlift Book Company.

Cover and text design by Betsy Stromberg
Contemporary project photographs by Scott Goodwin
Photography assistance by Kristin Rotondo

Library of Congress Cataloging-in-Publication Data

Kramer, Leah.
   The Craftster guide to nifty, thrifty, and kitschy
crafts : fifty fabulous projects from the fifties and
sixties / Leah Kramer.
      p. cm.
   Summary: "A full-color collection of fifty craft projects from the 1950s and 1960s, including new retro-
inspired crafts, from the founder of hipster craft
website, Craftster.org"—Provided by publisher.
   ISBN-13: 978-1-58008-747-6
   ISBN-10: 1-58008-747-7
   1. Handicraft. 2. Kitsch—United States. 3. Arts,
American—20th century. I. Title.
   TT157.K64 2006
   745.5—dc22
                                        2005035600

Printed in China
First printing, 2006
1 2 3 4 5 6 7 8 9 10 — 10 09 08 07 06

The Craftster Guide to
NIFTY, THRIFTY, AND KITSCHY
CRAFTS

Dedication

To Dave, who has been the biggest enabler of my creative addictions. To my parents and Rachel and Bryan, who put up with a daughter and a sister who was always leaving behind messy trails of glitter and fabric scraps. Finally, to all of the craftsters who provide me with endless inspiration every day.

Contents

ACCESSORIES

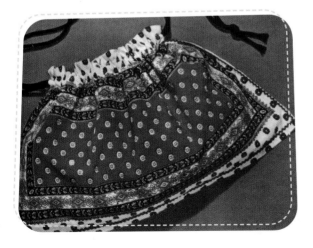

HOME

CLOTHING

NOVELTIES

HOLIDAY

Acknowledgments

Thanks to all the publishers of the vintage craft projects in this book who so generously allowed me to reprint these fabulous craft ideas. In particular, I'd like to thank *Pack-O-Fun* magazine and Aleene Jackson for allowing me to reprint so many of their projects and for being such pioneers of crafts in the 1950s and 1960s.

Thank you so much to the following people for contributing these vintage-inspired craft projects: Jordan Bach (Coffee Urn Lamp), Jen Corbett (Temptress Collar), Max Daniels (Sweater Teapot Cozy), Laura Dorato (Felt Animal Patches), Melanie Howe (Book Clutch Purse), and Trina Zerick (Crocheted Doll Face Fridgies).

And thank you to the following people for so skillfully crafting up versions of these vintage projects: Simone Alpen (Knitted Poodle Cozy, Bridge or Canasta Placemat Set, and Tote Bag Apron), Stacie Dolin (Bridge or Canasta Placemat Set), Laura Kluvo (Novel Necktie Apron), Dave McMahon (Felt and Foil Christmas Tree Ornaments, Foil Animals, Space-Age Party Accessories, Egg Carton Lantern, and Painted Glass Martini Set), Sharleen Morco (Crocheted Poodle Cozy), and Casandra's LeeLees Creations (Doll Cake).

A million thanks go to Lilly Ghahremani and Stefanie Von Borstel at Full Circle Literary for all of their hard work and moral support, Julie Bennett and Ten Speed Press for making this book possible, Betsy Stromberg for her beautiful design, and Scott Goodwin and Kristin Rotondo for the gorgeous photographs (and making sure each and every pom-pom was in place).

Last, but in no way least, to Dave McMahon, for whipping the vintage imagery into shape, for reading, rereading, and rereading again, and for the endless husbandly support.

INTRODUCTION

I have two serious addictions—rummaging through thrift stores, flea markets, and yard sales; and making stuff. In my rummaging escapades I'm always attracted to any artifact from the 1950s. There's this certain *je ne sais quoi* about things from that era—the furniture, appliances, and dishware with a space-age modern, yet retro, look; the graphics and ads dripping with treacle and saccharine turns of phrase; the depictions of an ideal home where strappingly handsome Dad sits in his armchair smoking a pipe and reading the paper while rosy-cheeked Mom, with perfectly coiffed hair, bakes a cake, an apron tied around her 20-inch waist; the humor of the cookbooks, with their supersaturated photos of glistening creamed corn casseroles and hot dogs wrapped in

cheese and then wrapped in bacon, and of course the liberal interpretation of the word "salad" to include a multitude of savory or sweet morsels suspended in molded gelatin . . . I could go on forever.

It's hard to say why I'm attracted to this era. It's not nostalgia, because I wasn't born until a couple of decades later. But it's just so appealing. Granted, I wouldn't have wanted to live in that era. I don't think I could keep up with the work involved in looking as polished as women were expected to. Then there's the idea of having a home so clean and orderly that you covered your teapot, toaster, and the extra roll of toilet paper in coordinated "cozies" (lest the prying eyes of your neighbors ever discover that you kept an extra roll near the toilet). Yet there's something unmistakably charming about it all.

I'm always thrilled when I encounter arts and crafts books from the 1950s and 1960s. The idea for this book came when my bookshelves started to sag under the weight of my collection. I'm fond of projects that make clever use of throwaways, as many old projects do. I enjoy the thriftiness and the extra ingenuity involved. But best of all, the crafts of that era are unmistakably retro and often hysterically kitschy—not on purpose!

Most of the projects in this book come right from vintage publications in my collection. A smattering of new projects with a similar sensibility are included. For the vintage projects, the original graphics are used, but the instructions have been rewritten to flesh out the steps, update the tools and materials involved (thank goodness the hot glue gun has since been invented), and add some of those pesky modern-day safety tips, all to make sure that you can actually make every one of these projects—if you dare!

QUICK GUIDE
to Craft Materials and Tools

*H*ere's information about materials and tools used in the projects in this book. It should also be handy for other craft projects you're inspired to take on.

ACRYLIC CRAFT PAINT

Craft supply stores carry loads of different kinds of paints. Acrylic craft paint comes in small plastic bottles in a huge range of colors. It's nontoxic and dries quickly, usually within an hour.

CHENILLE STEMS

This is the fancy term for what is also called pipe cleaners, which can be found at craft supply stores, usually in the kids' section.

CIGAR BOXES

Cigars are packaged in beautiful and sturdy boxes made of cardboard or wood. Because the boxes are so nicely made and useful for storing things, tobacco shops often save empty boxes and give them away or charge a small amount for them. Check your local tobacco shop or a convenience store or liquor store that sells cigars to see if they offer empty boxes.

CRAFT KNIFE

This is a general term for a cutting tool such as those made by X-Acto. You could also use a utility knife or a box cutter, but craft knives are better when you need to make detailed cutouts.

Craft knives are sold in art supply and craft supply shops.

CUTTING MAT

I recommend putting a "self-healing cutting mat" under whatever you are cutting with a craft knife. Made of special rubber that won't be penetrated by the knife as you cut, the mat is essential for protecting your work surface. You'll find the mats in art supply and craft supply shops.

DECOUPAGE GLUE

The word "decoupage" comes from *decouper*, which is French for "to cut up or to cut out." It's simply the process of cutting out images and gluing them all over something, such as a plain box or even a piece of furniture. Glue made specifically for decoupage is designed both to hold the paper cutouts on and to seal and protect your finished work. Mod Podge is a popular brand. It comes in a variety of finishes—glossy, matte, sparkly glitter, and even water-proof for outdoor use. It's also acid-free, which means that the paper cutouts won't be harmed by acids that deteriorate paper over time.

ELECTRIC DRILL

Some projects require a little drilling. If you're not experienced with a drill, don't use one without help from someone who is experienced. A few safety tips for using a drill are (1) always wear safety goggles and (2) place the item you are drilling into a vise, not in your hands—you don't want the spinning end of the drill to be anywhere near your hands. If you'd rather not dabble in the world of electric drills, ask the folks at your local hardware store if they will drill the item for you. I find that, as long as I'm buying other supplies from the store that day, they're usually happy to help out.

FABRIC GLUE

This is a special glue designed to hold two pieces of fabric together. It is sold in craft or sewing supply stores.

FELT

Felt comes in two varieties: acrylic and wool. Acrylic felt for crafts is often sold in 9 by 12-inch sheets in a huge range of colors and even prints. You'll find it at craft supply stores. Wool felt is more expensive but thicker and more durable. It's often sold by the yard in rolls 36 or 72 inches wide at sewing supply stores.

HOT GLUE GUN

Hot glue is terrific because it sets instantaneously: you apply it between two objects, and within seconds they are bonded. No need to hold them together as the glue sets (as can be the case with PVA glues—the polyvinyl acetate glues I call standard white craft glue and thick white craft glue). Like PVA glues, hot glue doesn't hold up for things that will be pulled a lot or receive other wear and tear. But it's great when you'd like to bond things instantly. It's also handy when you need a stronger hold between two awkwardly shaped objects—use a dab of hot glue just to hold them together, and then goop on a stronger glue and let it dry. Always be careful when using a hot glue gun—the glue really does get very hot.

PAPER-BACKED FUSIBLE WEBBING

A few projects call for paper-backed fusible webbing. Fusible webbing is a thin material that you place between two pieces of fabric that you want to join. When you iron the fabric "sandwich," the webbing sort of melts and bonds the fabric layers together. It's also handy for holding pieces of fabric together so that they won't shift position as you're sewing them. Paper-backed webbing allows you to iron the webbing onto one piece of fabric first, peel off the paper backing, and then iron the second piece of fabric on. You can find this webbing at sewing stores.

PHOTOCOPIER

A copier is handy for two things: (1) to enlarge or reduce an image or pattern piece you need to use in a bigger or smaller size; and (2) to make a color copy of an image you'd like to use in a project without destroying the original.

PILLOW STUFFING

Craft and sewing stores often carry bags of loose pillow stuffing for making stuffed toys or pillows. You have to buy a rather large bag of it, but you can reach into the bag and pull off as many pieces as you need for your project.

PLASTIC GEMS

Craft supply stores have a selection of plastic gems, or "rhinestones" in a variety of sizes and colors. They have flat backs, which make them fun and easy to glue to anything that needs a little sparkle.

SEWING MACHINE

These days very decent sewing machines can be bought for under $100. The small, inexpensive machines that sell for $29.95 or less "as seen on TV" are rumored to be more frustrating to work with than they're worth. If you don't own a sewing machine and you're considering buying one, try to borrow one from a friend or relative so you can see what you like and don't like about it. This will eventually help you choose your own.

SILICONE GLUE

Use silicone glue when you need a really strong hold. It's thick, dries clear, remains flexible after drying, and is waterproof. A common brand name is E-6000, and it can often be found in either craft stores or hardware stores. The downside to silicone glue is that its fumes are strong and not exactly good for you, so use it sparingly, and follow the directions on the back of the tube for ventilating your work space.

SPRAY PAINT

Spray paint comes in an aerosol-type can and is great for applying a thin, even layer of paint over three-dimensional objects that might be time consuming to paint with a paintbrush. Spray paint can be quite messy, so I recommend taking the object to be painted outside and laying it on newspapers. The paint can be found at hardware, art supply, and craft supply stores.

STABILIZER

A stiff fabric that gives shape to whatever you are sewing. You'll find stabilizer by the yard at sewing supply stores.

STANDARD WHITE CRAFT GLUE

White craft glue is very commonly used for crafts because it's nontoxic, doesn't have harsh fumes, and dries clear. An example is good old Elmer's glue. The technical term for this glue is

PVA (polyvinyl acetate). It's the best to use when you need to hold two porous materials together and the resulting object won't get a lot of wear and tear, so it doesn't require a really strong bond.

THICK WHITE CRAFT GLUE

There are lots of PVA (polyvinyl acetate) glues with different thicknesses and additives for different purposes. When a project calls for thick white craft glue, you'll want to find a brand of PVA glue that's purposely made to be thicker and less runny. Thicker glue is helpful when the two things you're gluing might start to slide apart with a thinner, runny glue. A good brand to look for is Aleene's Thick Designer Tacky Glue. Since this is a PVA glue, it's not recommended for things that require a really strong bond because they'll get a lot of wear and tear.

THROWAWAYS

Start paying more attention to what you put into your recycle bin and trash can, because the projects in this book have you using egg cartons, all kinds of plastic bottles, tinfoil, burned-out lightbulbs, tin can and yogurt container lids, and more. Once you get into the groove, you may have very little that you actually consider trash!

TIN SNIPS

Tin snips are specially made for cutting thin sheets of metal such as tin cans. Some are shaped like scissors, others like large wire cutters. They can be found in hardware stores. Note that kitchen shears will often work just as well in a pinch.

TRANSPARENT TAPE

This is the generic name for the kind of tape you use when wrapping a present. It comes in shiny and matte finishes. You can write on the matte variety.

WOOD GLUE

This glue is specially designed to hold pieces of wood together; it can even be stained or varnished. You can find it at hardware stores.

ACCESSORIES

CIGAR-BOX PURSE

Turn an old **CIGAR BOX** into a fashionable **PURSE!**

*C*igars often are packaged in beautiful and sturdy boxes made from cardboard or wood (see page 3). These instructions work for a standard-size cardboard cigar box (9$\frac{1}{2}$ inches long by 6$\frac{1}{2}$ inches wide by 2 inches high), but you can easily adjust the instructions if your box is a different size. For a variation on this purse, try using decorative paper instead of fabric, or adding a decoupage of fun cutout images, or leaving the cigar box in its beautiful unaltered state. In all of these variations you'll want to seal the purse to protect it, in case you're caught in the rain while you're carrying it. Waterproof sealer can be found in the glue or paint section of craft stores.

MATERIALS

1 standard-size (9 by 6$\frac{1}{2}$ by 2-inch) cardboard cigar box

Screwdriver

Measuring tape or ruler

Pencil

Scissors

1 yard printed cotton fabric, or enough to cover the cigar box

Standard white craft glue (see page 6), or fabric glue (see page 4)

8 binder clips

3 sheets (9 by 12-inch) craft felt (see page 4), or enough to line the inside of the box

1 U-shaped purse handle with screws for cigar-box purses (available at craft supply stores), or U-shaped drawer pull with screws (available at hardware stores)

1 jewelry box clasp (also called a hinged catch; available at woodworking supply stores), if the cigar box doesn't come with a clasp

1 yard pom-pom fringe

MAKES 1 PURSE

INSTRUCTIONS

1. If your cigar box has a clasp, carefully remove it with a screwdriver. You'll be covering the entire box in fabric, and you don't want to cover the clasp as well. Later, you'll reattach it.

2. With the measuring tape, measure the length and width of your cigar box. Add 2 inches to each measurement, and then mark and cut two rectangles of this size from the cotton fabric. (For this cigar box, the length is 9$\frac{1}{2}$ inches and the width is 6$\frac{1}{2}$ inches, so I cut two 11$\frac{1}{2}$ by 8$\frac{1}{2}$-inch rectangles.)

3. Measure the height of your cigar box, and measure from one corner all the way around the outside of the box to the same corner. Add 1 inch to each measurement, and then mark and cut one long rectangle of this size from the cotton fabric, to go around the height of the box. (For this cigar box, the height is 2 inches and the length all around is 32 inches, so I cut a rectangle 33 by 3 inches.)

4. To cover the cigar box with fabric, first turn it bottom side up. Spread some of the glue along the outer edges of the bottom. Center the fabric for the bottom over the glued area, and press the fabric down. Crisply fold the excess fabric over the four corners and sides of the box as if you were wrapping a present. Apply dabs of glue to the folded fabric corners as needed to hold them in place (the glue will dry clear, so you won't see it later). Secure the corners of the fabric with the binder clips while the glue dries (wait about 10 minutes, and then remove the clips).

5. To cover the top (lid) of the box, cut a 1-inch slit in the second fabric rectangle on each side edge, 1 inch from the intact corners as shown in the diagram. Spread some of the glue along the outer edges of the lid. Center the rectangle over the lid, with the slit fabric at the hinge side of the lid. Press the fabric down, crisply, folding the excess over the corners and three of the sides (not the hinge side) toward the inside of the lid. Apply dabs of glue to the folded fabric corners as needed to hold them in place, and secure the corners with binder clips (for about 10 minutes) while the glue dries. For the hinge side of the lid, spread some glue onto the flap of remaining fabric and press the flap over the back and around the back corners to the sides of the box.

6. To cover the sides of the box, fold under the raw edges of the long strip of fabric as you glue it around the height of the box. Hold the fabric in place with binder clips (for about 10 minutes) while the glue dries.

7. Next, line the inside of the box with the felt. This not only makes the inside look nice but also covers the edges of the cotton fabric that you folded and glued to the inside of the box. Open the box, and measure the length and width of the five interior surfaces to be covered. Measure and cut five pieces of felt to size. Measure the lid of the box, and then measure and cut one piece of felt slightly smaller than the lid. Glue all of the felt pieces in place. (The felt should stay in place as it dries so there's no need to wait before moving on.)

8. Attach the purse handle to the side of the purse that will have the opening and closing clasp. Center the handle vertically and horizontally, and then mark the location of each end of the handle, so you know where to place the screws. Insert the two small screws through the box from the inside and into the handle where you made your marks. (If you can't find a cigar-box purse handle with screws, a U-shaped drawer pull is a clever substitute; you attach it the same way.)

9. Now you'll reattach the clasp you removed, or add a new one if the box didn't come with one. Clasps come in two pieces and include screws.

The part of the clasp without the hinge goes on the side of the purse with the handle. The other piece screws into the inside top of the lid. Experiment with where the two pieces need to go, and mark the screw holes. Then screw the two pieces into place.

10. For a little extra kitschy flair, measure and cut two strips of pom-pom fringe (I used "mini" pom-pom fringe) to wrap around the top and bottom edges of the purse. Glue on the fringe, and let it dry for about 10 minutes. Once all the glue has dried, you've got yourself a kicky new purse!

CIGAR BOX PURSE

For young or old, a real conversation piece!

Use either a cardboard or wooden cigar box and cover with such fabric as wool (to match a favorite dress), felt, plastic or any heavy material.

To cover box, cut two pieces, each ¼" — ½" larger than top and bottom of box. Glue in place, overlapping excess to inside of cover, and up around sides from the bottom.

Next cut a strip of material slightly larger than the width of box and long enough to go around all four sides. Glue strip flush with bottom of box, overlapping excess to inside on three sides and trimming the fourth or back side to fit.

Line cover and inside, cutting each piece to fit before gluing.

Cut a cardboard handle, cover with material and attach with buttons. Add a button for closing also.

COVER TOP AND BOTTOM.

COVER SIDES

Cover it with fabric to match your FAVORITE DRESS!

Book Clutch PURSE

LOOK SMART and _literary_ with a hardcover **BOOK CLUTCH!**

*D*o you have some beautiful old hardcover books lying around that you've already read a million times and will never read again? You can make them into unique clutches. Or look in thrift stores and used bookstores to find a great-looking book for this project. You'll want a thick tome to give your clutch enough room to hold your necessaries.

MATERIALS

1 hardcover book with a spine at least 2 inches wide

Craft knife (see page 3)

Measuring tape or metal ruler

1 piece thick cardboard at least as long and wide as the book's spine

Hot glue gun (see page 5)

Paper-backed fusible webbing (see page 5)

Iron and ironing board

Cotton fabric to line the purse

Pencil

Heavy paper

Sewing machine (optional; see page 6)

Needle and thread

Adhesive Velcro dots for the clutch closure

Ribbon and buttons or buckles

MAKES 1 CLUTCH PURSE

INSTRUCTIONS

1. Remove the pages from the book by carefully cutting lengthwise on the inside cover along the spine and toward the pages with the craft knife.

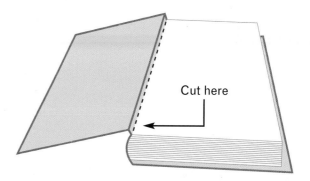

Cut here

2. Measure the inside length and width of the spine. Cut the cardboard to those measurements.

3. Apply hot glue to one side of the cardboard, and attach it to the inside of the spine (see page 16). Press the two together for 20 seconds while holding the cardboard flat. (This will strengthen the spine, which will be the bottom of the clutch.)

4. Open the cover flat on a surface, inside up. Measure the length and width of the cover, and

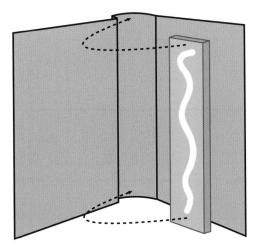

cut a piece of the fusible webbing to size. Place the fusible webbing on the cover, paper side up. Lightly iron the webbing onto the cover for 15 seconds (check the instructions on the webbing package for the appropriate heat setting).

5. Cut a piece of the fabric for the lining 1/4 inch longer and wider than the measurements of the cover. Place the fabric right side down on the ironing board, fold 1/4 inch in on each edge, and press with the iron (see below). The lining will now be 1/4 inch shorter than the book cover in width and length.

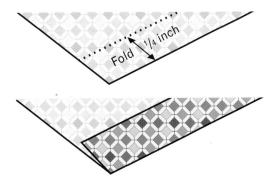

6. Peel the backing from the fusible webbing, and place the fabric on top, wrong side down. Slowly circle the iron around the center of the fabric to fuse it to the webbing on the covers and spine, but leave the top and bottom edges unfused for now.

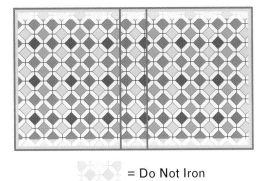

= Do Not Iron

7. Holding the spine down on the table, close the two sides of the book cover. Measure the width of the spine. Next, hold the book sides open as far as you'd like the clutch purse to open, and measure this width. Then measure the length of the cover sides, from spine to top. Add 1/4 inch allowance to each of these measurements, and draw a pattern for the purse side panel on the heavy paper. (Your pattern should look like a triangle with the point cut off.)

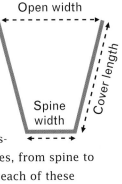

8. Cut out the pattern, and use it as a stencil to mark and cut four pieces from the lining fabric (two for each side panel of the purse). Place two pieces right sides together, fold them in half lengthwise, and iron them to form a crisp crease. Unfold, and sew the pieces together, $1/4$ inch in from the top edge (the wider width of the triangle). Turn the pieces right side out, fold both layers of each long edge of the triangle over $1/4$ inch, and press. You'll soon attach this $1/4$-inch allowance along the long sides of the panel into the sides of the book. Repeat the folding, pressing, and sewing with the other two pieces of fabric to create the second side panel.

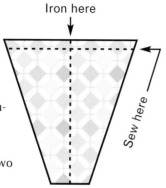

Iron here

Sew here

9. Apply hot glue to the bottom (narrower width) of one side panel, and slide it under the fabric on the spine. This secures the bottom of your triangle between the fabric and the cardboard. Repeat for the other side panel.

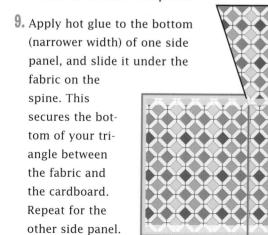

10. Apply hot glue to the inside right and left edges of the book cover, and slide the folded edges of the side panel triangle between the cover and the fabric webbing. Repeat for the other side panel. Press the edges of the cover to fuse the lining to the cover at the edges.

11. Glue a piece of the Velcro to the top-center inside edge of each side of the purse so you can snap the purse closed. Glue the ribbon and buttons or buckles to the outside covers of the purse to decorate them. Throw in your wallet, cell phone, and keys, and you're ready to go!

POPSICLE STICK PURSE

FINALLY, A PURSE THAT'S BOTH **SWEET** AND **COOL!**

*I*n case you're wondering—no, you don't have to eat 250 Popsicles in order to make this purse. Not even 125 double Popsicles. Take a trip to your local craft supply store, and check the kids' section to find bags of Popsicle sticks. This project involves a lot of glue, and you're quite likely to get it all over your work space, so pick a surface where you can easily wash the glue off, or work on a plastic tray. You'll want to allow the glue to set between each row, which makes this a great project to do while working on other projects. You can leave your purse in its natural Popsicle-stick glory, or use any kind of paint, stain, or varnish made for wood. Glue some kitschy embellishments on to complete the look. Wood glue (see page 7) is recommended for this project because not only is it specifically designed for wood but it also works well with wood finishes.

MATERIALS

Wood glue (see page 7)

250 Popsicle sticks

2 decorative upholstery nails

7 inches thin round sewing elastic

18 inches craft wire for the handle

Beads (enough to string on and fill about 15 inches of wire)

Paint, stain, or varnish suitable for wood and a suitable brush (optional)

Fake flowers or other decorative kitchy items

MAKES 1 PURSE

INSTRUCTIONS

1. To create the base of the purse, glue 11 Popsicle sticks together side by side to form a rectangle (see figure 1). Allow the glue to set for a couple of minutes. Glue 1 stick perpendicular to the row of sticks and close to one end of the row; glue 1 more stick close to the opposite end (see figure 1). Turn the base over (right side up); it should look like figure 2 from the top.

2. Next, build up the sides and body of the purse. With the base right side up and its top row of sticks running horizontally, glue 4 Popsicle sticks to the base at a 45-degree angle to the horizontal sticks in a diamond shape (see figure 3, row A). Allow the glue to set for a couple of minutes between each row. Glue 4 more sticks on top of the diamond shape, but in a square aligned with the base sticks (see figure 3, row B). Repeat the diamond and square rows alternately for 28 rows, but on each row, move

the sticks out about $1/8$ inch so the purse gets wider as you build. After 28 rows (including the first two), continue to alternate diamond and square shapes for 28 additional rows, but move each row inward by $1/8$ inch to decrease the size of the purse again. Not including the base, you'll have 56 rows altogether.

3. To make the lid, follow step 1 above. Then push one of the decorative upholstery nails firmly into each end of the sixth stick in the top of the lid. Allow the nail head to stick up just enough so that the elastic can slip under it. Cut the elastic in half, and tie one half around the middle of the top few sticks of the purse body on one side of the purse; keep the knot on the inside of the purse and the loop on the outside. Tie the other half of the elastic the same way on the opposite side of the purse. Set the lid on the purse body with the decorative nails next to the two loops, and slip the elastics over the nails to close the purse.

4. To make the handle, thread the beads onto the craft wire, leaving $1^1/2$ inches of empty wire at each end. Loop one end of the wire around the top 2 rows of sticks on a side of the purse that doesn't have an elastic loop, then thread the wire back through the closest bead. Bend the wire and its beads into a loop handle, and attach the other end to the opposite side of the purse in the same way.

5. Decorate your purse with paint, stain, or varnish, if you like, and glue on the kitschy items for a truly cool look.

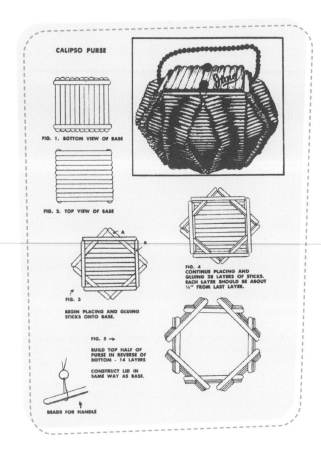

CALIPSO PURSE

FIG. 1. BOTTOM VIEW OF BASE

FIG. 2. TOP VIEW OF BASE

FIG. 3

BEGIN PLACING AND GLUING STICKS ONTO BASE.

FIG. 5 →

BUILD TOP HALF OF PURSE IN REVERSE OF BOTTOM - 14 LAYERS

CONSTRUCT LID IN SAME WAY AS BASE.

BEADS FOR HANDLE

FIG. 4
CONTINUE PLACING AND GLUING 28 LAYERS OF STICKS. EACH LAYER SHOULD BE ABOUT 1/8" FROM LAST LAYER.

SPOOL-KNIT *Monogram*

With an empty thread spool, knit enough rope for projects *galore!*

*W*hen I was a kid, my mother bought me a small tube-shaped plastic loom with which I create really, really, really long knitted ropes. I never did think of anything to do with those ropes, nor did I ever stop to think why the loom was called a "spool knitter," until I encountered this project in a vintage craft book. These looms where originally made by pounding four nails into an empty wooden spool of thread. You learn something new every day! After you create ropes with your spool knitter, you can coil them and stitch them together to create loads of nifty things, from purses to trivets to chair pads. If you spool knit with thicker materials, like rug yarn, nylon stocking strips, or strips of fabric, you can even coil the resulting rope to make a rug—just use a larger spool with a big center hole.

MATERIALS

Hammer

4 brads (also called 18-gauge nails)

1 empty wooden spool of thread

Worsted-weight yarn

Large sewing needle

Scissors

Plain-colored cotton or canvas purse

Needle and thread (to match the yarn)

1/2 yard (1/2-inch-wide) satin ribbon

**MAKES 1 SPOOL KNITTER AND
1 LETTER MONOGRAM**

INSTRUCTIONS

1. Hammer the four brads evenly spaced around the top of the spool near the hole in the middle, leaving enough of the nail sticking up so that two thickness of your yarn can fit on it easily without slipping off.

2. Feed the loose end of the yarn through the hole in the spool from the top until 6 inches of yarn hang out the bottom of the spool. Using the yarn at the top of the spool, wrap firmly but with some give around one brad and then diagonally around the opposite brad to form a figure eight. Next, wrap around a third brad and make the figure eight with the fourth brad.

3. To begin knitting the rope, pass the yarn on the outside of the brad counterclockwise from the last brad you wrapped; keep the yarn between the head of the brad and the loop of yarn already on the brad. With the needle, pull the bottom loop of yarn over the top yarn and off the brad. This will leave one loop on the

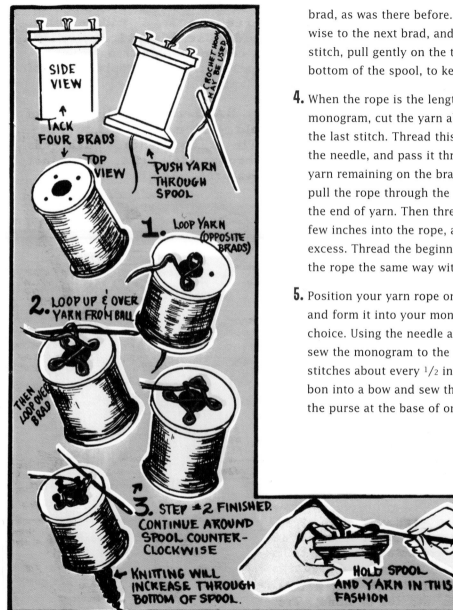

SIDE VIEW

↑
TACK FOUR BRADS
↓

TOP VIEW

PUSH YARN THROUGH SPOOL

CROCHET HOOK MAY BE USED

1. LOOP YARN (OPPOSITE BRADS)

2. LOOP UP & OVER YARN FROM BALL

THEN LOOP OVER BRAD

3. STEP #2 FINISHED. CONTINUE AROUND SPOOL COUNTER-CLOCKWISE

KNITTING WILL INCREASE THROUGH BOTTOM OF SPOOL.

HOLD SPOOL AND YARN IN THIS FASHION

brad, as was there before. Move counterclockwise to the next brad, and repeat. After each stitch, pull gently on the tail coming out of the bottom of the spool, to keep the knitting taut.

4. When the rope is the length you want for your monogram, cut the yarn about 6 inches from the last stitch. Thread this last bit of yarn into the needle, and pass it through each loop of yarn remaining on the brads. Slip the loops off, pull the rope through the spool, and tighten the end of yarn. Then thread the end of yarn a few inches into the rope, and cut off the excess. Thread the beginning tail of yarn into the rope the same way with the needle.

5. Position your yarn rope on top of the purse and form it into your monogram letter of choice. Using the needle and matching thread, sew the monogram to the purse using small stitches about every 1/2 inch. Tie the satin ribbon into a bow and sew the bow to the top of the purse at the base of one of the handles.

Towel HANDBAG

THIS
*Bag's on the
Square!*

*T*ake a trip to a thrift store to find yourself a gaudy and colorful vintage towel for this project. Note that the instructions require some basic knowledge of how to sew with a sewing machine or by hand, including hemming and making a tuck. The handle of the bag is attached with four bone rings, which are actually made from plastic and are available at craft or sewing supply stores.

MATERIALS

Scissors

1 (5$\frac{1}{2}$-inch-square) piece heavyweight stabilizer (see page 6)

Sewing machine (optional; see page 6)

Needle and thread

1 (22-inch-square) piece lightweight plastic or vinyl tablecloth

1 bath towel, cut into a 22-inch square

4 ($\frac{3}{4}$-inch-diameter) bone rings

2 yards narrow decorative cord

MAKES 1 HANDBAG

INSTRUCTIONS

1. Cut the square edges of the stabilizer into a circle. Sew the stabilizer to the center of the plastic along the edge of the circle.

2. Turn in and hem any raw edges on the towel. Lay the plastic square, stabilizer side down, on the wrong side of the towel, and sew around all four edges.

3. To define the shape of the purse bottom, stitch a narrow tuck (raised fold) on the outside of the towel and plastic around the circle of stabilizer by pinching the layers together and stitching close to the fold.

4. Bring two adjacent corners of the towel (and plastic) square together to fold one top edge in half, with the fold away from the bottom circle of the handbag, and sew the edges together from the fold for 5$\frac{1}{2}$ inches. Repeat for the other three sides of the towel.

5. Sew a bone ring to each of the top corners. Thread one end of the cord through each of the bone rings, then tie the ends of the cord into a knot. The purse closes by pulling the cord.

Glovely Lovely COIN PURSE

Lost a glove and feel bereft?

Make this from the one that's left!

*T*here was a time when special occasions meant fancy white gloves for women and girls. If you were a thrifty and crafty lady, you'd look for things to make with an orphan glove when you'd lost its mate. Here's a fun idea. Today you can find vintage ladies' gloves (often already missing a mate) at flea markets and antique shops. Because gloves tend to get yellow with age, you may want to spruce them up with a washing in bleach. This cute coin purse can store some change, a handkerchief, and a few keys. Note that you'll need to know some basic sewing techniques, including blanket-stitching, overcasting, tacking, and attaching snaps.

MATERIALS

Scissors or craft knife (see page 3)

1 white cotton ladies' glove

Embroidery thread (in a contrasting color) and needle

White sewing thread and needle

1 (5-inch-long) key chain (available at hardware stores)

3 sew-on snaps (available at craft or sewing supply stores)

Sequins and beads for decoration

MAKES 1 COIN PURSE

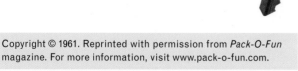

INSTRUCTIONS

1. To make a pocket for your coins, cut a slit through one layer of the glove on the back side at base-of-the-thumb level. Turn under the raw edge closest to the fingers and blanket-stitch a hem with the embroidery thread. Sew the other edge of the slit to the palm of the glove with an overcast or zigzag stitch to prevent fraying. To close the pocket at the bottom, stitch through both layers of the glove across the base of the fingers.

2. Turn the glove palm-side up, and fold the thumb across the palm. With the sewing needle and thread, tack down just the tip of the thumb to the palm of the glove. Fasten the key chain over the thumb.

3. Now make the final closings. On the back side of the glove, sew one side of one snap in the center of the sewn line at the base of the fingers and the other side of the snap at the wrist (when you fold the glove over just above the coin pocket slit, you'll be able to snap it closed). To make an extra compartment for a handkerchief, sew two additional snaps inside the wrist.

4. Decorate your coin purse with embroidery, sequins, and beads.

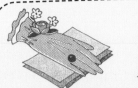

Glovely Lovelies

Lost a glove and feel bereft?
Make these from the one that's left!

Paperweight

For a zany, "handy" desk accessory, fill a light-colored glove with plaster of Paris mixture, pouring it inside while someone holds the glove open. Work the plaster into the fingers and fill to wrist. Pinch in at wrist and allow to dry. When dry, sponge or brush off excess plaster on outside of glove. Glue a bead to ring finger and tie flowers at wrist.

Novelty Coin Purse

To make a pocket for coins in this unusual purse, cut a slit across back of glove in position shown. Turn under raw edge closest to fingers and blanket stitch with contrasting yarn. Sew other edge to palm, overcasting to prevent fraying. To close pocket at bottom, stitch across base of fingers.

Now turn glove over, fold thumb across palm and tack down just the tip to palm of glove. Fasten a key chain or loop of braided yarn over thumb. Decorate your purse with yarn, blanket stitched around fingers and embroidered around cuff.

All that remains now are the final closings. Fold glove over just above coin pocket slit and attach a snap to base of fingers and at wrist. One or two additional snaps inside wrist will give you an extra compartment for a hanky.

Cosmetic Holder

Here's a handy holder for all that purse clutter! Cut and remove the palm of a glove, including thumb. Overcast raw edges with yarn. The back part of the glove forms a flap which can be embroidered as desired.

Coin Purse

Cosmetic Holder

32   PACK-O-FUN

Felt Flower APPLIQUÉS

Add these flowers
to your poodle skirt,
and you're ready to
MAKE THE SCENE!

*A*fter you've mastered the three flower styles in this project, you can experiment with different petal shapes for an infinite variety of flowers. Then glue them onto barrettes, pin them onto a jacket or skirt, glue them all over a boring piece of furniture—add them to anything that needs a little pizzazz. You can either use glue to assemble the flowers or hand-stitch them with a few stitches wherever gluing is mentioned.

MATERIALS

Pencil

Heavy paper

Scissors

2 (9 by 12-inch) sheets craft felt (see page 4) in two contrasting colors

Thick white craft glue (see page 7)

Small binder clips

Mini pom-poms, beads, sequins, or other trimmings

MAKES 3 FLOWERS

INSTRUCTIONS FOR THE DAISY

1. Trace the large and small daisy patterns onto heavy paper, cut them out, and use them as stencils to mark and cut out the felt. Cut six large petals of one color and six small petals of the contrasting color.

2. Glue a small petal onto each large petal. To cup the combined petal, place a line of glue at the base of the petal, as shown by the shaded area on the pattern. Fold the petal in half vertically and use a binder clip to hold it in this position until the glue has set (about 10 minutes).

3. Cut a 1-inch-diameter disk of either color of felt. Glue the petals onto the disk in a circle. Glue a pom-pom in the center of the flower, and let the glue dry thoroughly.

INSTRUCTIONS FOR THE POINSETTIA

1. Trace the large and small poinsettia patterns onto heavy paper, cut them out, and use them as stencils to mark and cut out the felt. Cut six large petals of one color and six small petals of the contrasting color.

2. Follow steps 2–3 in the Daisy instructions to construct the flower, but don't glue a pom-pom in the center.

3. To make stamens, cut thin strips of felt, and glue them to the center of the flower.

INSTRUCTIONS FOR THE ZINNIA

1. Trace the inner and outer zinnia petal patterns in all three sizes onto heavy paper, cut them out, and use them as stencils to cut out the felt. Using the outer patterns, cut eight large petals, eight medium petals, and seven small petals in one color. Using the inner patterns, cut eight large petals, eight medium petals, and seven small petals in the contrasting color. Glue each inner petal to its contrasting outer petal.

2. Follow step 2 in the Daisy instructions to cup and glue the petals.

3. Cut a 1-inch-diameter disk of either color of felt. Glue the eight large cupped petals onto the disk in an evenly spaced circle. Allow the glue to set, about 10 minutes. Glue the eight medium cupped petals on top of the previous row of petals in an evenly spaced circle. Allow the glue to set again, about 10 minutes. Finally, glue the seven small cupped petals on top of the previous row of petals in an evenly spaced circle. Glue a pom-pom in the center of the flower, and let the glue dry thoroughly.

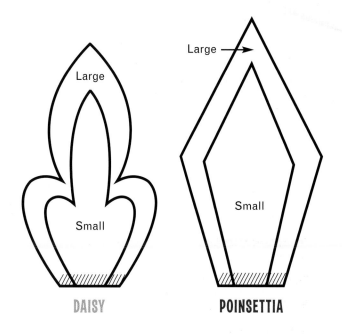

DAISY

POINSETTIA

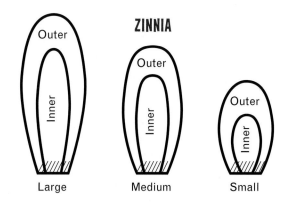

ZINNIA

Large

Medium

Small

Felt ANIMAL PATCHES

Spruce up
A PLAIN CARDIGAN
OR SKIRT WITH A
FUN AND FUZZY
felt patch!

*C*raft felt is so appealing—the colors are bold and the texture is warm and fuzzy. These iron-on felt animal patches will positively pop out of anything you attach them to—purses, sweaters, coats, anything made of fabric. They are also great little gifts that you can whip up in no time and then give to friends to iron onto their own clothes.

MATERIALS

Pencil

Heavy paper

Scissors

Children's books featuring simple animal shapes (optional)

$1/2$ yard paper-backed fusible webbing (see page 5)

1 (9 by 12-inch) sheet craft felt (see page 4)

Iron and ironing board

Embroidery thread and needle

MAKES APPROXIMATELY 5 PATCHES

INSTRUCTIONS

1. Draw some freehand animal shapes on heavy paper, and cut them out to use as guides. If you need inspiration, look for examples in the children's books.

2. Cut a piece from the fusible webbing the same size as the sheet of felt, and iron it onto the felt according to the manufacturer's instructions. Do not remove the backing paper from the webbing yet.

3. Using your paper cutouts as guides, cut animal shapes out of the felt. Conveniently, the paper-backed webbing makes the felt easier to cut.

4. Peel off the paper backing, and decorate the animals by embroidering eyes, mouths, and whatever else you want onto them with the embroidery thread. Now your little felt patch is ready to be ironed onto whatever you choose. If the item you are ironing the patch onto specifies a low heat setting (as fabric that contains polyester does), be sure to follow that setting.

Slip-On TOOTHBRUSH Bracelet

Don't give old toothbrushes **THE BRUSH OFF** just because they're **LONG IN THE TOOTH!**

I was really excited to encounter this project, because, although it's from 1962, I know that people are still making toothbrush bracelets all these years later. Write a message in alphabet pasta or let your imagination go wild with sequins and beads to personalize your bracelet.

MATERIALS

Pot of water and stove

1 plastic toothbrush

Pliers

Thick heatproof work gloves

2 pairs of tongs

Standard white craft glue (see page 6)

Beads, sequins, or letter-shaped pasta for decoration

MAKES 1 BRACELET

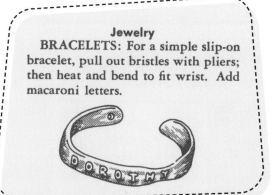

Jewelry
BRACELETS: For a simple slip-on bracelet, pull out bristles with pliers; then heat and bend to fit wrist. Add macaroni letters.

INSTRUCTIONS

1. Place the pot of water on the stove over high heat.

2. Remove the bristles from the head of the toothbrush with the pliers.

3. When the water is boiling, place the toothbrush in the water to soften the plastic. The amount of time needed to soften the plastic varies. To see whether the toothbrush is pliable, put on the heatproof gloves, grab each end of the toothbrush with a pair of tongs, and try to bend it slowly. If it doesn't bend easily, return it to the boiling water for a few minutes more.

4. When the toothbrush is warm enough to bend, use the tongs to bend it into a circle, leaving a gap of at least 1 inch so it can slip easily onto your wrist but won't fall off. (Shape the toothbrush on a heatproof surface, not on your wrist, because the plastic will be very hot.)

5. When the toothbrush has cooled, glue beads, sequins, or letter-shaped pasta to the outer side for decoration.

Charming CHARM Bracelet

Every girl can be more *charming* with her own unique CHARM BRACELET!

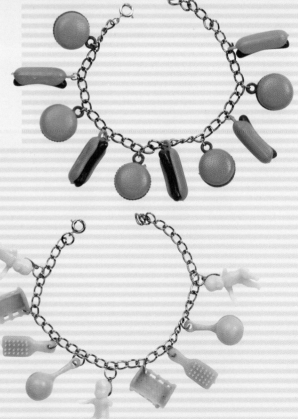

*C*raft stores and bead shops have all the jewelry "findings" (hardware for necklaces, earrings, and bracelets) you need for this bracelet: chains, clasps, and jump rings (small metal rings with a break that can be twisted open and clamped closed using needle-nose pliers). You'll find small charms or toys in gumball machines, toy stores, cake decorating shops, and train or dollhouse miniature shops. If a small toy doesn't have a loop to attach it to the bracelet, you can glue on a jewelry finding called a "drop loop"—a small metal pad with a loop built into it. Use a strong silicone-based glue to attach the drop loop to make sure that it will hold securely.

MATERIALS

Needle-nose pliers

Jump rings (available at craft or jewelry supply stores or bead shops)

8 to 12 plastic charms and tiny toys

Glue-on drop loops (if needed) and silicone glue (see page 6)

8 inches cable chain (available at craft or jewelry supply stores or bead shops)

1 bracelet clasp (available at craft or jewelry supply stores or bead shops)

MAKES 1 CHARM BRACELET

INSTRUCTIONS

1. Using the needle-nose pliers, carefully twist open one jump ring, and slide a charm onto it. (Glue a drop loop to any charm or toy that has no loop before attaching the jump ring; let the glue dry.)

2. Slide the jump ring onto one of the links in the cable chain, and close the jump ring with the pliers.

3. Repeat with the rest of the charms, spacing them as you'd like. Leave 1 inch free of charms at one end of the chain; this makes the bracelet adjustable for various wrist sizes. Using the needle-nose pliers, attach the clasp to the opposite end of the chain with a jump ring.

FLOWER POWER EARRINGS

PLAYFUL EARRINGS FROM PLASTIC BOTTLES!

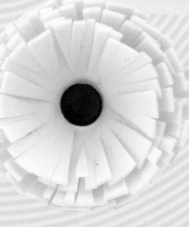

*D*on't let those plastic bottles fill up a landfill somewhere. Instead, cut them up to make fetching flower earrings. They are both thrifty and fashionable. "Findings" are the little supplies needed to make jewelry (see page 37). For earrings, they are the hooks or posts that attach the earring to your ear. Craft supply stores and bead or jewelry-making stores sell them.

MATERIALS

Pencil

Heavy paper

Scissors

2 (or more) brightly colored empty plastic bottles

Bowl of hot water

Towel

Knitting needle (optional)

Silicone glue (see page 6)

4 plastic gems (see page 6) for the center decoration

4 earring findings

MAKES 2 PAIRS OF EARRINGS

INSTRUCTIONS FOR THE ASTER EARRINGS

1. Trace the aster pattern onto the heavy paper, and cut it out. Use the cutout as a stencil to trace and cut out three circles from one of the plastic bottles, but cut one circle slightly larger and one slightly smaller than the stencil.

2. To make a fringe, cut partway in from the edge of each circle at about 1/8-inch intervals.

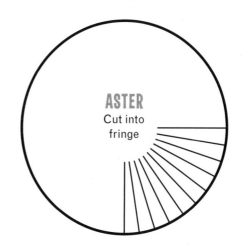

ASTER
Cut into
fringe

3. Place each fringed circle into the bowl of hot water to soften the plastic slightly, about 2 minutes. Remove the circle from the water, dry it with the towel, and curl each fringe over the pencil or knitting needle.

4. Glue the plastic circles together at their centers, largest on the bottom, smallest on the top, so the fringe creates three layers of petals. Glue a plastic gem in the middle of the fringe on the top layer.

5. Glue an earring finding to the back of the flower.

6. Repeat for the other earring.

LOTUS

INSTRUCTIONS FOR THE LOTUS EARRINGS

1. Trace the lotus pattern onto the heavy paper, and cut it out. Use the cutout as a stencil to trace and cut out two flower shapes from a plastic bottle, but cut one slightly smaller than the other.

2. Place each flower shape into the hot water for about 2 minutes to soften the plastic slightly. Remove the shape from the water, dry it with the towel, and curl each petal over a pencil or knitting needle.

3. Glue the smaller flower on top of the larger flower. Glue a plastic gem in the center of the petals on the top flower.

4. Glue an earring finding to the back of the flower.

5. Repeat for the other earring.

CIGAR-BOX *Makeup Kit*

MAKE UP A *cigar box* **FOR YOUR MAKEUP!**

*H*ere is another way to use an empty cigar box. You can decorate the cigar box first by painting it, decoupaging it, or covering it with paper or fabric as shown in the Cigar-Box Purse project (see page 10). If the cigar box is appealing just as it is, then leave it alone.

MATERIALS

2 small sponge paintbrushes

Acrylic craft paint in two contrasting colors (one for the outside and one for the inside)

1 cardboard or wooden cigar box

Favorite comic books and magazines

Scissors

Decoupage glue (see page 4)

1 sheet (8$\frac{1}{2}$ x 11-inch) decorative paper (optional)

1 yard ribbon

4 tiny screws (available at woodworking supply stores)

Tiny screwdriver

Hot glue gun (see page 5)

Small mirror (available at craft supply stores and drugstores)

MAKES 1 MAKEUP BOX

INSTRUCTIONS

1. Using one of the sponge paintbrushes, paint the outside of the cigar box with the acrylic paint, and let it dry thoroughly according to the directions on the paint bottle.

2. From your comic books and magazines, cut out images you want to use, and experiment with arranging them on the lid of the box. When you have a layout you like, use the second sponge paintbrush to place decoupage glue on

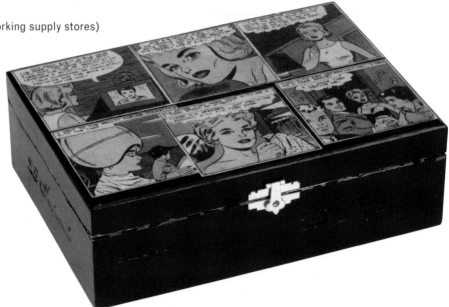

the back of each image, and lay them on the lid, smoothing out any bubbles and wrinkles in the paper.

3. Using the sponge paintbrush, apply a layer of decoupage glue over the entire box, one side at a time, allowing the glue to dry before moving on to another side. This seals the paper cutouts and gives the box a consistent sheen.

4. When the box is dry, use the second color of acrylic paint to paint the inside of the box. Let the box dry thoroughly.

5. If your jewelry box is wooden, like the one shown, cut strips from the decorative paper and glue them to the inner lip of the box for a little extra flair. (Cardboard cigar boxes are thinner than wooden boxes and don't have the inner lip.)

6. Cut two pieces of ribbon to attach to the box and lid, so that the lid will stay open and be tilted back slightly. For the cigar box shown (10 by 8 by 3 inches), each ribbon needed to be 12 inches long, but test the length with your own box. Using one of the tiny screws at each end, attach the ribbons to the front inside edges on each side of the box and the lid, as shown in the photograph, using the tiny screwdriver.

7. Using the hot glue gun, glue the mirror to the inside of the lid.

Make-Up Box
Cover cigar box as desired and cement two diagonal straps of twill tape or seam binding between top rim of box and lid so lid has a slight backward slant when open.

Reinforce straps with tape for security. Cement a small mirror inside the lid.

Add a colorful fabric or plastic ruffle around box.

MOLDED RECORDS

Put a
NEW SPIN
on an old stack of
RECORDS!

*H*ere are some wild ways to reuse that forlorn batch of records stashed in your closet. If you don't have any old records kicking around, you can often find some at thrift stores, yard sales, and flea markets (for as little as 25¢ each). A few of the projects below involve heating a record in the oven on a form (such as a bowl) until the record gets slightly soft and can be shaped. After you've mastered this technique, use your imagination to think of forms you can use to shape the records in different ways—casserole dishes, pie pans, metal cake pans in various shapes, and so on. A trip to a discount kitchen supply store will yield some interesting possibilities. Just make sure that any form you use is oven-safe. And remember that the hole in the center of the record will still be there, so don't put any liquids in your bowls. The last two projects are clever ideas that do not require heat.

Ruffled Bowl and Nut Dish

MATERIALS

Baking sheet

Aluminum foil

Ovenproof bowl (slightly larger in diameter than LP record)

1 (12-inch) LP record (for ruffled bowl)

Heatproof gloves or oven mitts

1 (45-rpm) record (for nut dish)

1 metal bowl (slightly smaller in diameter than 45-rpm record; for nut dish)

MAKES 1 RUFFLED BOWL AND 1 NUT DISH

INSTRUCTIONS FOR THE RUFFLED BOWL

1. Preheat the oven to 350°F.

2. Line the baking sheet with the aluminum foil. Set the ovenproof bowl right side up on the baking sheet, and center the LP record on top of the bowl. Place the baking sheet in the oven, and allow the record to heat just until it is pliable, about 2 to 3 minutes or when the record just begins to sink into the bowl a bit. Be careful not to keep the record in the oven for more than a few minutes; it should be heated only enough to soften it slightly.

3. Wearing the heatproof gloves, remove the baking sheet from the oven, and slowly push the center of the record down into the bowl. Ruffles will form in the record as you do this,

creating a bowl out of the record itself. It's tricky to get the ruffles completely even in size and symmetrical, but the more you make, the better you'll get at it. Luckily, uneven ruffles look just as charming. *Note:* The record will harden quickly as it cools; if it hardens too much while you are working on it, or if you want to change the shape, just put it back into the oven for a few more minutes to soften again.

INSTRUCTIONS FOR THE NUT DISH

You can make individual snack dishes and trinket bowls by following the directions for the Ruffled Bowl using 45-rpm records instead. Use a smaller metal bowl that's closer in size to the finished product you'd like.

Ruffled Dishes

Place a record over a tin can and when it becomes pliable, quickly set it into a pie pan. Rotate the pan on the rack while forming the ruffles. For a planter, use a pan with higher sides.

RUFFLED DISHES

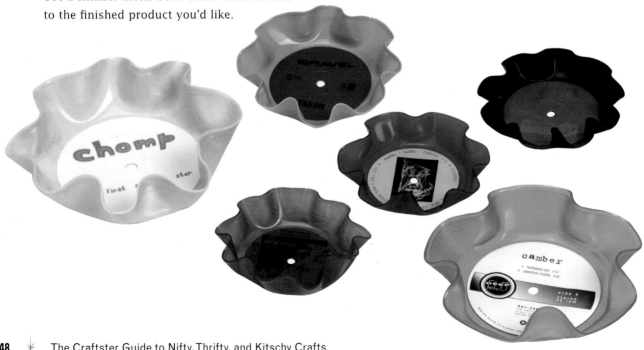

Lazy Susan

MATERIALS

1 baking sheet

Aluminum foil

2 (12-inch) LP records

1 empty tin can (4 inches high and no more than 3$^1/_2$ inches in diameter)

Heatproof gloves or oven mitts

1 (9-inch) pie pan

1 (6-milimeter) bolt, nut, and washer set (available at hardware stores)

1 small ovenproof bowl

1 (45-rpm) record

MAKES 1 LAZY SUSAN

INSTRUCTIONS

1. To make the base of the lazy Susan, follow the softening instructions for the Ruffled Bowl but use one of the 12-inch records and the tin can to form a deep, narrow bowl. Remember to wear the heatproof gloves.

2. Soften the second 12-inch record, and mold it in the pie pan so it stays mostly flat and turns up only at the outer edges. This will look more like a tray than a bowl.

3. When the two pieces are cool, attach them together as follows. With the pie pan record right side up (open side up), insert the bolt down through the record's hole. Place the washer on the bolt (on the bottom side of the bowl). Flip the tin can bowl upside down (open side down) to form the base of the lazy Susan. Put the bolt through the hole in the tin can record, and attach the nut to the end of the bolt (inside the tin can record). The two records are now connected, with the washer between them so that the lazy Susan can spin.

4. If you'd like, create a small nut dish with the 45-rpm record to place on top of the lazy Susan.

Napkin Holder

MATERIALS

1 (12-inch) LP record

Cutting mat (see page 4), or cutting board

Metal ruler

Utility knife, or box cutter

Safety goggles

Sandpaper

Hot glue gun (see page 5)

1 plastic napkin holder, or a small cardboard box big enough to hold napkins

MAKES 1
NAPKIN
HOLDER

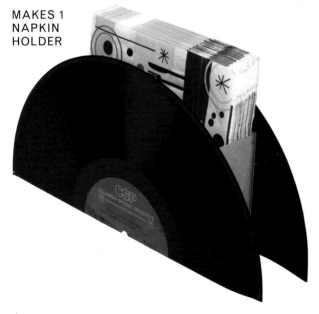

INSTRUCTIONS

1. Place the record on the cutting mat. With the metal ruler and the utility knife, carefully score the record right down the middle (the diameter) a few times from one edge to the other. You don't have to make a very deep cut, but the more you score, the easier time you'll have.

2. Put on the safety goggles, and snap the record in half at the line you scored. It should break cleanly, but safety goggles will protect you just in case small pieces do fly off.

3. Use the sandpaper to smooth the edges and corners of the record.

4. Using a hot glue gun, glue one half of the record (straight edge down) to each side of the plastic napkin holder, and allow the glue to dry.

Napkin Holder

Cover a box of suitable size with decorative paper. Break a record in half by scoring it with a knife along the center line, then striking sharply along a table edge. Spray with metallic paint and glue the halves to the sides of the box.

Record Clock

MATERIALS

1 clock kit (available at craft and woodworking supply stores)

1 (12-inch) LP record

Electric drill (see page 4), if necessary

MAKES 1 CLOCK

INSTRUCTIONS

1. Clock kits come with everything you need to make a clock except the face. Follow the easy kit directions to snap the clock parts together.

2. Fit the clock mechanism into the center of the record. If you find that the hole in the record needs to be slightly larger, use the electric drill to widen it. This is a great way to immortalize a favorite album or favorite single. It looks especially cool if you use an LP made of colored vinyl.

Painted Glass Martini Set

Paint some **PANACHE** onto your glassware for **CHEERIER COCKTAILS!**

*T*his neat little trick for painting designs onto glasses came from a 1950s craft book. It's great if you can't draw freehand, because it lets you easily use an existing image as a guide. The old craft book called for a special kind of paint that had to be hardened, after you applied it to the glass, using a kiln or an oven. Luckily, now there is special glass paint that's dishwasher-safe, and you don't need to bake it. Amble off to a craft store that has a large supply of craft paints to find this kind of paint.

MATERIALS

Pencil and paper

Books, magazines, photocopier, or computer and printer, for designs (optional)

Transparent tape (see page 7)

Set of clear martini glasses

Small paintbrush

Paints for use on glass (available at craft supply stores)

Clear glass martini shaker

MAKES 1 SET OF GLASSES AND 1 SHAKER

INSTRUCTIONS

1. To reproduce a design onto the martini glasses and the glass shaker, choose a simple original image that you draw by hand on paper, or copy one from a book or magazine, or print out one from clip art made available on the computer.

2. Tape the image to the inside of one martini glass with the design facing outward. Using the paper image as a guide, paint the design onto the outside of the glass. Repeat for the other glasses and the martini shaker.

ETCHED GLASSWARE

AMAZE YOUR FRIENDS by creating **CUSTOM-ETCHED** vases and glasses!

*E*tching cream for use at home has been around since at least the 1950s. Today, you can easily find it at craft supply stores. Make sure that you follow the directions carefully and wear rubber gloves (such as dishwashing gloves) when using it. Create your own design to etch, or copy one from a book or magazine, or go for a traditional holiday motif, or use letters to make a personal statement.

MATERIALS

Pencil

Adhesive vinyl paper (contact paper)

Cutting mat (see page 4)

Craft knife (see page 3)

Glass vase

Rubber gloves

Small paintbrush

Glass-etching cream (available at craft supply stores)

Adhesive vinyl letters (available at craft supply stores)

Cocktail glasses

1-inch-wide masking tape

MAKES 1 VASE AND 1 SET OF COCKTAIL GLASSES

INSTRUCTIONS FOR THE VASE

1. Draw or trace onto the adhesive vinyl paper the shapes you want to etch. Place the paper on the cutting mat, and carefully cut out and remove the shapes using the craft knife. To create a mini stencil, cut a generous rectangle in the remaining adhesive vinyl around each area where you cut a shape out.

2. Remove the backing from the adhesive paper stencils, and carefully position each stencil on the vase. Press the adhesive down firmly around the cut-out areas, so no etching cream will seep under the paper.

3. Wearing rubber gloves and using the paintbrush, apply the etching cream according to the manufacturer's instructions on the cut-out areas of each stencil. Allow the cream to sit on the vase for as long as the bottle indicates; then rinse it off thoroughly. Peel off the stencils, and you'll have a fashionable retro-inspired vase like none other!

INSTRUCTIONS FOR THE COCKTAIL GLASSES

1. Using adhesive vinyl letters, spell out a word or phrase on a set of cocktail glasses. Press the letters down firmly, and use masking tape to create a rectangle around the letters.

2. Follow step 3 on page 55 to apply the etching cream within the area of the masking tape. When you rinse off the etching cream and remove the tape and letters, you'll have a rectangular area of etched glass with the word or phrase spelled out in smooth glass. This technique provides endless possibilities for personalized gifts.

Nifty Storage *with* BABY FOOD JARS

PUT THOSE LITTLE
baby food jars
TO WORK FOR YOUR
creative projects!

$\mathcal{M}$ ake an eye-catching craft supply shelf for beads and sequins, or a kitschy storage place for your kitchen spices. Organize your pens and pencils or condiments with a neat jar set, or make a customized snow globe. Before using the jars, clean them well, and soak them for 30 minutes in warm water with a little dish soap to remove the labels. If the labels don't fall off by themselves, scrub them off with a scouring pad.

Supply Shelf

MATERIALS

4 baby food jars with screw-off lids, emptied and cleaned

1 standard wooden shelf (at least 12 inches wide), including brackets, mounting strips, and screws

Ruler or measuring tape

Hammer

8 nails (shorter in length than the thickness of the shelf)

Screwdriver

MAKES 1 SHELF

INSTRUCTIONS

1. Unscrew the lids from the baby food jars. Lay the shelf on a work surface, and space the lids, top down, evenly across the board.

2. Hammer each lid in place with two nails spaced about $1/2$ inch apart. Turn the board over so the lids are facing down, and using the brackets and mounting strips, mount the shelf on the wall at a height that's handy for you to reach.

3. Fill each jar with one kind of supplies, and simply screw the jars into their lids.

Triple Pencil or Condiment Holder

MATERIALS

Acrylic craft paint (see page 3)

Paintbrush

3 (6-ounce) baby food jars or 3 small mayonnaise jars, emptied and cleaned

Electrical tape

Brightly colored yarn, string, or raffia

MAKES 1 PENCIL HOLDER

INSTRUCTIONS

1. Paint the jars on the inside only, and allow the paint to dry completely. (To make a condiment holder for ketchup, mustard, and relish, follow these instructions but don't paint the insides of the jars.)

2. Gather the jars into a triangular group, and wrap them together securely with the electrical tape.

3. Decorate the jars (to cover the tape) by wrapping them with the yarn, string, or raffia. Wrap the necks of the jars to hide the screw-top ridges.

Snow Globe

MATERIALS

Small plastic figurines

1 baby food jar with a lid, emptied and cleaned

Silicone glue (see page 6)

Water

Clear corn syrup

Glitter

MAKES 1 SNOW GLOBE

INSTRUCTIONS

1. Glue the plastic figurines to the inside of the jar lid using the silicone glue. Allow the glue to dry completely according to the package instructions.

2. Fill the baby food jar with 2 parts water and 1 part corn syrup. Leave about $1/4$ inch of room at the top. Add some glitter to the water mixture.

3. Screw the lid on and give your snow globe a test run. If you think your globe needs more glitter, just add more. When you're happy with the amount of glitter, spread the silicone glue on the threads of the jar and screw on the lid tightly to seal the jar permanently.

Supply shelf and triple holder copyright © 1961. Reprinted with permission from *Pack-O-Fun* magazine. For more information, visit www.pack-o-fun.com.

EGG CARTON LANTERN

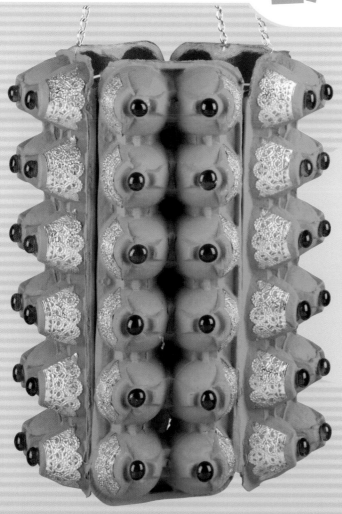

YOU'LL **SCRAMBLE** TO MAKE THIS **LAMP!**

*H*ere's another project that will get you thinking about your trash in a whole new way. It requires a hanging lantern lamp kit, which is simply a lightbulb and a switch attached to a very long cord. You can find these kits in hardware stores, lighting supply stores, and places that sell lots of paper lanterns. Start saving those egg cartons right away.

MATERIALS

Craft knife (see page 3)

5 to 6 (dozen-size) cardboard egg cartons

Thick white craft glue (see page 7)

Stapler

Paintbrush

Acrylic craft paint

Flat-backed glass floral marbles (available at craft or floral supply stores), gold paper doilies, plastic rhinestones, or sequins for decoration

Scissors

Heavy craft wire (available at hardware or craft supply stores)

Thin craft wire (available at hardware or craft supply stores)

3 (8-inch-long) pieces lightweight chain (available at hardware stores)

Hanging lantern lamp kit

MAKES 1 LANTERN

INSTRUCTIONS

1. Using the craft knife, cut the lid from each egg carton, leaving a $1/2$-inch strip of flap at each side. Fold the flaps inward and glue the flap of one carton to the flap of a second carton. Staple along this edge for extra strength. Fasten all of the cartons together in this manner, with their insides facing in, to complete a circle of cartons. The number of egg cartons you use depends on how large in diameter you want your lantern to be.

2. With the craft knife, carefully make a small slit between each pair of egg cups in each carton. Holding the outside of each carton facing you, gently bend the carton away from you to open up the slit areas.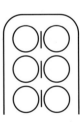

3. Paint the outside of the lantern with the acrylic paint and let it dry completely, about 1 hour.

4. With the craft knife, neatly cut a small hole into the bottom of each egg cup. Glue a glass marble over each hole; the light will shine through the marble. Cut triangles from the

gold doilies and glue them to the edges of the cups. Glue on jewels or sequins for decoration.

5. Using part of the heavy craft wire, form a circle that fits snugly into the top of the lantern about $1/4$ inch from the top edge, and twist the wire ends to hold the circle together. Fasten the circle to the top of the lantern by  threading short pieces of the thin craft wire through the top edges of the egg cartons in a few places and wrapping the wire around the circle. Form a second circle from the remaining heavy craft wire, and attach it to the bottom edge of the lantern in the same way.

6. To hang the lamp, fasten one end of each of the lengths of chain to the top wire circle using the thin craft wire. Space the chains evenly around the wire circle. Fasten the three opposite ends of the chain lengths together with more thin craft wire (see figure 3).

7. Assemble the hanging lantern lamp kit following the manufacturer's instructions, and insert the lamp into the egg carton lantern. Hang it up from the chains at the top, plug it in, and let there be light!

PLEATED
PUNCH-CARD LAMP SHADE

PUNCH CARDS—
THE COMPUTER-AGE SCRAP!

*I*f you can get your hands on a stack of old punch cards (try eBay or other online auction websites), make this clever lamp shade and watch the light flicker through the tiny holes. These instructions assume that you are using a standard-size punch card (approximately $7^3/_8$ by $3^1/_4$ inches). If you don't have access to old punch cards, try using decorative paper that lets light through in an interesting way, such as translucent handmade paper with embedded flowers or funky-colored vellum (similar to tracing paper but thicker). Make sure the paper you choose creases well. This pattern will make a shade about 10 inches high.

MATERIALS

Measuring tape

1 standard cone-shaped lamp shade, no more than 7 inches from top to bottom edges

Scissors

1 (2 by 15-inch) piece cardboard

Hot glue gun (see page 5)

About 40 computer punch cards, or an equivalent amount of decorative paper

Transparent tape (see page 7)

Pencil

Paper

Rickrack or ribbon

MAKES 1 LAMP SHADE

INSTRUCTIONS

1. Using the measuring tape, measure the circumference of the inner top rim of the lamp shade. Trim the piece of cardboard so the length matches the circumference of the lamp shade. Using the hot glue gun, attach the cardboard to the inner top rim of the lamp shade to create a collar. (Hot glue works well here because it sets instantly.)

2. Using the circumference measurement from step 1, add one-third of that length to the total measurement, and round up to the nearest inch. (For instance, if the collar measures $12^1/_2$ inches, one-third of that measurement is about $4^1/_8$ inches. Add $12^1/_2$ to $4^1/_8$, and round up to 17 inches.)

3. To make a pleated strip to slip over the collar, trim 2 punch cards to an even 7 inches long, and tape them together end to end. Continue to trim and tape, until the row of cards matches or exceeds the length you found in step 2 above. (If you're using decorative paper instead, cut a strip $3^1/_4$ inches wide by the length you

calculated in step 2.) Fold the strip of cards every $^1/_2$ inch as if you were folding a fan. Tape the ends together to make a ring, and glue it to the collar using the hot glue gun. Count the number of pleats you have in the collar (you'll need to know this for steps 4 and 6).

4. Trace template A onto a piece of paper. Cut it out, and use it as a stencil to trace and cut pieces from the punch cards (or the decorative paper), cutting as many A-shaped pieces as you have pleats in the collar. Flop the pattern, and cut an equal number of punch cards (or pieces from the decorative paper). Tape the A-shaped pieces together on their long sides, straight edge to straight edge and diagonal to diagonal, keeping all the tab ends at the top. You'll be alternating flopped and unflopped pieces. When the pieces are all assembled, fanfold them with the diagonal edges pointing inward (see diagram A). Tape the last piece to the first to form a ring.

5. Bend the tabs at the tops of the A-shaped pieces out slightly, and glue them to the bottom of the pleated collar around the cone-shaped lamp shade.

6. To make the frill around the top of the shade, trace and cut template B onto a piece of paper. Cut it out, and use it as a stencil to trace and cut B-shaped pieces from the punch cards or decorative paper. Cut as many pieces as you have pleats in the collar. Bend each piece in

half lengthwise, with the folded edge on the outside (see diagram B). Tape all the pieces together, keeping the tabs at the bottom; tape the last piece to the first to make a ring. Bend the tabs out slightly, and glue them to the top of the pleated collar so the frill extends $^1/_2$ inch above the collar.

7. Glue the ribbon or rickrack around the top and bottom of the pleated collar to hide the tabs that attach the pleated shade and the top frill.

PLEATED LAMP SHADE

PLEATED COLLAR

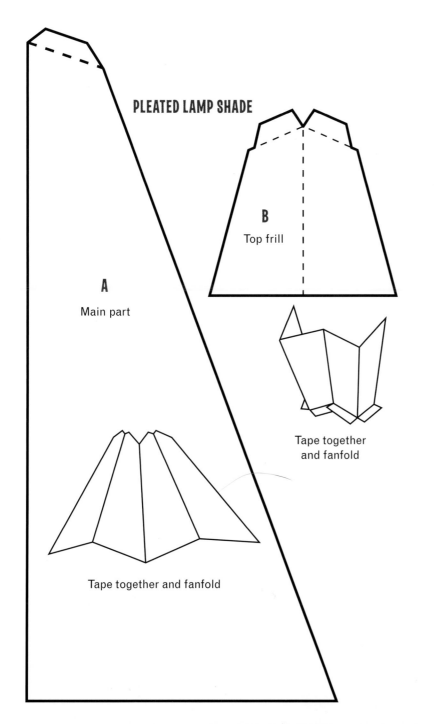

A

Main part

Tape together and fanfold

B

Top frill

Tape together and fanfold

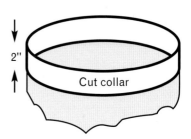

2"

Cut collar

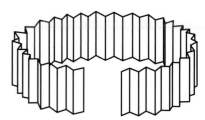

Fanfold for strip around collar
and tape ends

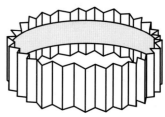

Glue pleated ring to collar

Lamp with *Plastic* Flower *Panache*

Welcome to the
Age of Plastic!

Add a touch of
Bloom
to your room!

These days, artificial flowers are usually made of silk or other fabric and look very realistic. In the fifties and sixties, however, they were often made of plastic and had an appealing extra-fake look. To replicate the 1950s aura, you can still find campy plastic flowers, if you know where to look. Flea markets, thrift stores, and yard sales may yield some vintage plastic flowers, but did you know that some cake decorating shops and restaurant supply stores carry a plentiful supply of new plastic flowers designed for reusable food-friendly adornment? Use them to decorate not only lamps, but also picture frames, vases, note cards, and whatever else strikes your fancy. Simply glue blossoms all over these plain items with a hot glue gun.

MATERIALS

Scissors

About 50 plastic flowers, or other artificial flowers

Lamp with a clear glass base that is meant to be filled (available at craft supply stores)

Hot glue gun (see page 5)

Lamp shade

MAKES 1 LAMP

INSTRUCTIONS

1. Snip off the blossom part of several of the plastic flowers. Screw off the bottom of the lamp, and fill the base with flower blossoms.

2. Using the hot glue gun, attach more blossoms around the edge of the lamp shade.

Coffee Urn LAMP

This lamp is
**GROUNDS FOR
EXCITEMENT!**

Old coffee urns like the one this lamp is made from are easy to find if you keep an eye out at thrift stores, yard sales, and church sales. The more outdated the coffee urn, the more likely it is to come in a fabulous color like avocado green. You transform the urn into a base for the lamp, and buy a lamp kit to complete the project. For kitschy lamp shades, see pages 64 and 68.

MATERIALS

1 coffee urn

Sponge

Screwdriver

Pliers

Lamp kit

Electric drill and 3/8-inch drill bit (see page 4)

Lightbulb

Lamp shade

Standard white craft glue (optional; see page 6)

MAKES 1 LAMP

INSTRUCTIONS

1. Discard (or find some clever use for) any removable parts, such as the metal coffee strainer, that may still be inside the coffee urn. Clean the urn with a damp sponge, and let it dry thoroughly.

2. Remove the spigot from the lower front part of the urn by unscrewing the screw that holds it on. Then twist apart the spigot itself. Inside there will be a rubber stopper. Pull this out with the pliers, reassemble the spigot, and reattach it to the urn. (Now you'll be able to thread the lamp cord through the spigot in step 3.)

3. Open the lamp kit, and find the cord. Thread the exposed wire end of the cord through the spigot from outside the urn to the inside.

4. Remove the decorative knob on the lid of the urn (you can probably just twist it off). The hole where this knob was connected is where you'll insert the bottom part of the lamp kit (called the "threaded nipple"). The hole is probably too small for the threaded nipple, so enlarge the hole using the drill and bit. (If you're not comfortable using an electric drill, ask someone who's experienced for help, or bring the lid to your local hardware store and ask if someone will drill it for you.)

5. Assemble the lamp kit by following the manufacturer's instructions exactly (even if they vary from those outlined below), and fit it into the coffee urn. Most instructions go basically like this:

- Insert the threaded nipple from above into the hole in the coffee urn lid so that the lower end hangs down at least $1/4$ inch, then screw a "thread locknut" onto each side (top and bottom) of the threaded nipple to hold it in place.

- Slide the "lamp harp" onto the threaded nipple. The harp is what holds up the lamp shade.

- Screw on the "socket cap." Now take hold of the exposed-wire end of the cord that you threaded through the spigot in step 3, and draw it up through the threaded nipple.

- Follow the instructions and diagram in the lamp kit to attach the wires of the cord to the terminal screws on the lightbulb socket. Your lamp should now be wired properly, and you can add a lightbulb and a lamp shade.

6. To be extra thrifty, you can make a "finial" out of the knob you removed from the coffee urn lid. At the top of a typical lamp harp there is a standard-size screw onto which you can screw a standard-size finial. If the knob happens to fit right onto this screw, then lucky you! If not, you may need to enlarge the hole in the knob with the drill, apply some glue inside the hole, and (after putting your lamp shade on) fit the knob onto the screw at the top of the harp. Plug in the lamp, sit back with your morning coffee, flip the switch, and bask in the glow of your swanky new coffee urn lamp.

Tidy COVERS

Make your
commode
commodern!

*H*ere are a couple of kitschy toilet lid covers, one covered with flower petals, the other with ruffles from an old shower curtain. After creating one of these, add a matching toilet paper cozy for the extra roll of paper that you put on the back of the toilet, and you're on your way to a true 1950s-style bathroom. Note that this project will go faster with a sewing machine, but it also requires some hand-sewing and knowledge of basic techniques, including threading elastic through a casing, gathering a fabric edge, ruffling with a basting stitch, and sewing on a ruffle.

MATERIALS

Measuring tape

Scissors

2 large terry cloth bath towels

Sewing machine (optional; see page 6)

Needle and thread

1 yard (1/2-inch-wide) sewing elastic

For the Petal Cover

4 to 6 pom-poms

For the Ruffled Cover

1 plastic shower curtain

1 fake flower

MAKES 1 PETAL AND 1 RUFFLED TOILET SEAT COVER

INSTRUCTIONS FOR THE PETAL COVER

1. Measure the length and width of your toilet lid. Cut two circles or ovals of terry cloth a couple of inches larger than the lid.

2. On one circle or oval, measure 1 1/2 inches in from the edge all the way around, and cut out the center to leave a 1 1/2-inch-wide ring. Position the oval and the ring right sides together. Stitch around the outer edge about 1/2 inch in from the edge. Turn the right sides out to hide the stitching. Sew the inner edge of the towel ring to the oval about 1/2 inch in from the inner edge. Leave about 2 inches unsewn for threading in the elastic. Your casing will look nicely finished along the outer edge and unfinished along the inner edge. The unfinished edge will be hidden when you place the cover on the toilet seat.

3. Measure a piece of elastic that is about 2 inches shorter in length than the circumference of the toilet lid. Thread the elastic through the casing, and sew one end of the elastic to the other to

form a circle. Hand-stitch the small opening in the casing closed.

4. To make the petals, cut 12 (5-inch) squares and 22 (3-inch) squares from the leftover towel. Cut each square into the petal shape shown in the diagram. To make the petals fluffy and three-dimensional, hand-stitch two petals together,

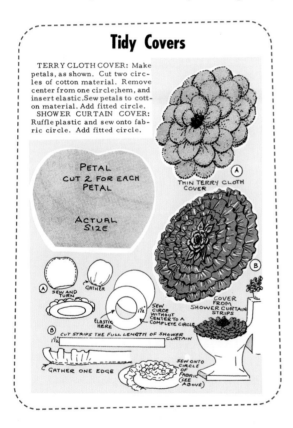

leaving the bottoms of the petals open. Turn the petals inside out, and then gather the bottom edge. This leaves you with 6 large and 11 small petals.

5. Hand-stitch the petals onto the toilet seat cover, starting at the outside and overlapping rings of petals until the whole circle or oval is covered. Finally, hand-stitch the pom-poms to the center of the flower.

INSTRUCTIONS FOR THE RUFFLED COVER

1. Follow steps 1–3 of the Petal Cover to create a terry cloth toilet seat cover.

2. With scissors, cut 1½-inch-wide lengthwise strips from the shower curtain. Ruffle each strip by sewing an easy in-and-out basting stitch all along one edge down the strip and then pulling gently on the end of the thread to pucker the material.

3. Using a running stitch (see resources section), hand-sew the ruffled strips onto the toilet seat cover in a spiral, starting in the center.

4. Hand-sew the flower to the center of the cover.

Sweater TEAPOT COZY

A cozy new life for an old sweater!

*I*n this project, you'll take an old wool sweater, felt it, and then cut it up and sew it into a fabulous cover to keep your pot of tea warm. Choose a sweater that's at least 60 percent wool or other animal fiber, such as alpaca or cashmere (acrylic and cotton yarns won't felt). Thrift stores are great places to find old sweaters. To felt a knit piece, you agitate it in hot water and color-safe detergent so that the yarn thickens significantly. You may have accidentally felted a wool sweater by letting it slip by you into the hot-water wash on laundry day—when you took it out, your sweater had shrunk to half its size and was twice as thick. If felting is done properly, the edges won't unravel when you cut the felted fabric.

MATERIALS

1 sweater (at least 60 percent wool)

Washing machine

$1/8$ cup color-safe detergent

Photocopier

Scissors

Straight pins

Tapestry needle

About $1^1/_2$ yards worsted-weight yarn in a color contrasting with the sweater color

1 (9 by 12-inch) piece felt in a color contrasting with the sweater color

1 sheet paper-backed fusible webbing (see page 5)

Colorful buttons (optional)

MAKES 1 TEAPOT COZY

INSTRUCTIONS

1. Throw the sweater into the washing machine with the detergent, and set the dials for a hot-water wash cycle with a high amount of agitation. If you don't want the wool to become too thick, check on the sweater every few minutes. If you want the wool to be very thick, you may have to run it through the cycle more than once. After the sweater is felted to the thickness you prefer, let it air-dry completely.

2. Using the photocopier, enlarge template A on page 79 until two pieces are big enough to cover your teapot. (The fabric should stretch a bit; for an 8-cup teapot, the pattern should measure about 9 inches in height and 11 inches in width.) Cut out two enlarged template A pieces and one template B piece. Pin them to the felted sweater, and cut them out.

3. Pin the two pieces of A together, right sides facing out. Fold B in half, right side out, and pin it between the two pieces of A at the top.

4. Thread the tapestry needle with the yarn and, starting at the bottom left side, hand-stitch the two pieces of A together using a running stitch (thread the yarn in and out at regular intervals). When you reach B (the tab) at the top, stitch through the two pieces of A and the two pieces of B and stitch around the edges of the tab for decoration. Continue stitching the two pieces of A together down the right side for 4 inches and then stop. At this point, stitch only through the front piece of A for 4 inches to create an opening for the teapot spout. Once you have created the opening, resume stitching through both pieces of A until you reach the bottom ride side. To create matching decorative stitches along the spout opening on the back side of the cozy, draw the yarn up through the stitches on the inside of the cozy and stitch through the back side of A only. Cut the yarn and secure the end with a knot on the inside of the cozy.

5. Decorate your cozy by adding an appliqué of felt in a contrasting color (using the paper backed fusible webbing: cut a piece to match your appliqué, iron it onto the appliqué, remove the paper backing, and iron the appliqué with the webbing side down onto the cozy), or by embroidering a design in the contrasting yarn, or by sewing on colorful buttons. Invite some friends over, brew up a pot of tea, and show off your new cozy!

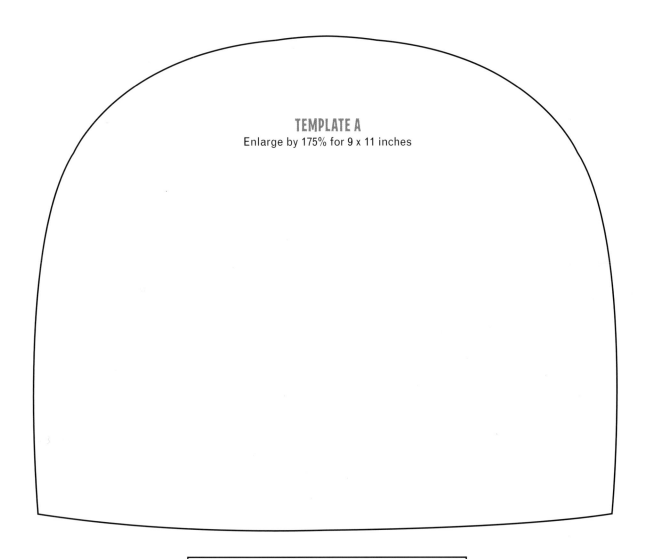

TEMPLATE A
Enlarge by 175% for 9 x 11 inches

TEMPLATE B

POWDER ROOM Poodle

A **charming** COVER-UP
FOR THE EXTRA ROLL OF TISSUE
IN YOUR BATHROOM!

*W*hat could be more quintessentially 1950s than a toilet paper cozy in the shape of a poodle? This fun cozy can be either knitted or crocheted. Instructions for both techniques are given, but you need to know how to knit or crochet to follow the patterns. You make the body starting from the bottom, the head starting from the top, and the nose starting from its black tip. Then you fashion the pom-poms for the poodle's topknot, ears, legs, and tail, put them all together, add facial features, and this pooch is ready to guard your toilet paper in style.

MATERIALS

For the Knitted Poodle

2 ounces Coats & Clark Red Heart Medium Yarn (or equivalent worsted-weight yarn)

Size 10 (U.S.) knitting needles

6 stitch markers

Tapestry needle

For the Crocheted Poodle

4 ounces Coats & Clark Red Heart Medium Yarn (or equivalent worsted-weight yarn)

Size H crochet hook

For Either Poodle

Scissors

2 yards worsted-weight black yarn

1 (1¹/₂-inch-wide) piece of cardboard

Embroidery needle

Loose pillow stuffing (optional; see page 5)

2 small black buttons

²/₃ yard elastic thread

ABBREVIATIONS

beg = beginning

ch = chain

dc = double crochet

dec = decrease

inc(s) = increase(s)

k = knit

MC = main color

p = purl

rnd = round

sc = single crochet

sl st = slip stitch

sp(s) = space(s)

st(s) = stitch(es)

tog = together

* = repeat whatever follows the * the number of times specified

( ) = do what is in parentheses the number of times specified

MAKES 1 TOILET PAPER COZY

INSTRUCTIONS FOR THE KNITTED POODLE

Gauge

3 sts = 1 inch; 6 rows = 1 inch

Body

1. With MC yarn, cast on 43 sts. Row 1: Work in stockinette st (k 1 row, p 1 row) for 4½ inches, ending with a p row.

2. Row 2: K1 (place a marker on the needle, k2tog, k5) 6 times.

3. Row 3: Sp across, slipping the markers to the other needle.

4. Row 4: K1, *slip marker, k2tog, k to next marker. Repeat from * to end of row.

5. Repeat rows 3–4 until 13 sts remain. P across, removing markers.

6. Next row: K1 (k2tog) 6 times. Cut the yarn, leaving a 10-inch tail. Thread the tail into the needle, and draw it through the remaining 7 sts. Pull the yarn taut. Sew the ends of the rows neatly together to make a center back seam for the poodle body.

Head

1. With MC, cast on 6 sts. Row 1: K in front and back of each st across (the row will have increased to 12 sts).

2. Row 2: P across.

3. Row 3: K across, increasing 6 sts evenly spaced (total will be 18 sts).

4. Repeat rows 2–3 once more (total will be 24 sts).

5. Work even for 11 rows (rows 6–16).

6. Row 17: (K2tog) 12 times (total will be 12 sts).

7. Row 18: P across.

8. Row 19: K across, increasing 6 sts evenly spaced (total will be 18 sts).

9. Row 20: P across. Bind off loosely. With long tail of yarn, sew side edges together to make a center back seam.

Nose

1. With the black yarn, cast on 5 sts. Row 1: K in front and back of each st across (the row will have increased to 10 sts). Cut and fasten off the black yarn, and attach MC yarn.

2. Row 2: P across.

3. Continue in stockinette st for 6 more rows. Bind off loosely. With tail of yarn, sew side edges together. Go to the instructions for finishing the poodle on page 84.

INSTRUCTIONS FOR THE CROCHETED POODLE

Gauge

5 dc and 5 sps = 2 inches; 2 rnds = 1 inch

Body

1. With MC yarn, ch 4. Join last ch to 1st with sl st to form ring.

2. Rnd 1: Ch 4, (dc in ring, ch 1) 11 times. Join to 3rd ch at beg of rnd with sl st.

3. Rnd 2: Ch 4, dc in back loop only of joining sl st of round 1 below, ch 1, dc in back loop of next dc below, ch 1; * in back loop of next dc below (dc, ch 1) 2 times (to inc 1 sp), dc in next dc below, ch 1. Repeat from * around. Join with sl st as before.

4. Rnds 3–5: Work same as rnd 2, increasing 6 sps evenly around (total will be 36 sps on rnd 5).

5. Rnds 6–13: Work same as rnd 2, omitting incs. Cut yarn, and fasten off at end of last rnd.

Head

This is worked in a spiral rather than joining and chaining at the beginning and end of rows. If you are a beginner crocheter, mark the end of each row with a stitch marker so you have a reference point.

1. Ch 2. Rnd 1: Make 6 sc in 2nd ch from hook.

2. Rnd 2: 2 sc in each sc of rnd 1 (total 12 sts).

3. Rnd 3: *Sc in 1st sc below, 2 sc in next sc to inc. Repeat from * around (total 18 sts).

4. Rnd 4: *1 sc in next 2 scs, then 2 sc in next sc, to inc 6 sc evenly spaced. Repeat from * around (total 24 sts).

5. Rnd 5: *1 sc in next 3 scs, then 2 sc in next sc to inc. Repeat from * around (total 30 sc).

6. Rnds 6–11: Work in sc without increasing.

7. Rnd 12: *1 sc in next 3 scs, then dec over next 2 scs. Repeat from * around (total 24 sts).

8. Rnd 13: *1 sc in next 2 scs, then dec over next 2 scs. Repeat from * around (total 18 sts).

9. Rnd 14: Work in sc without decreasing.

10. Rnd 15: *1 sc in next sc, then dec over next 2 scs. Repeat from * around (total 12 sts).

11. Rnd 16: Work without increasing. Cut yarn, and fasten off.

Nose

Now you will switch to the black yarn and start to work the nose. This is also done in a spiral. To switch colors you tie the new yarn onto the old piece of yarn and then weave the ends in later.

1. Starting with the black yarn, ch 2. Rnd 1: Make 6 sc in 2nd ch from hook. Cut yarn, and fasten off.

2. Attach MC, and work rnd 2 same as rnd 2 of head.

3. Rnds 3–6: Sc in each sc around. Cut yarn, and fasten off at end of last rnd. See instructions for finished the poodle below.

FINISHING THE POODLE

1. To create the three pom-poms for the head, cut a strip of cardboard 1¹/₂ inches wide, and wind the MC yarn 100 times around that width; cut the end of the yarn. Cut a short piece of yarn, slip it between the strands of yarn and the cardboard, and tie its ends together tightly, gathering the strands together. Cut the strands at the end opposite the tie, and comb and brush the cut ends to fluff them out. Repeat to make two more pom-poms.

2. To create the five pom-poms for the legs and tail, follow step 1 above, but wind the yarn around the cardboard only 60 times. Repeat to make four more pom-poms.

3. Use black yarn and the embroidery needle to stitch the mouth on either side of the nose. You can do this with a stem stitch or by embroidering a few chain stitches.

4. Stuff the head and nose with the remaining yarn or pillow stuffing. With the MC yarn, sew the nose to the head. Sew on the buttons for eyes. Sew one pom-pom to the top of the head and one on either side for the ears. Sew the lower edge of the head to the top of the body. Sew the pom-pom legs and tail to the body.

5. Slide the body over a roll of toilet paper. Fold the elastic thread in half and draw it through stitches at the lower edge of the body, using the needle or crochet hook. Pull the ends of the elastic tight to fit over the roll of paper, and tie the ends together.

Powder Room Poodle copyright © 1962 Coats & Clark, Inc.

Mermaid
BATHROOM TISSUE COVER

This delightful **water nymph** isn't just for decoration— she hides a roll of bathroom tissue from **prying eyes!**

$\mathcal{W}$ hat could be more camp than a mermaid-themed toilet paper cozy? The instructions from the vintage craft book that published this project didn't include directions for making the mermaid, but with a little glue, some polymer clay, and a lot of retro inspiration, I'm sure you can come up with just the right siren to sit atop your new cozy.

MATERIALS

Measuring tape

1 (1/2-gallon) bleach bottle

Craft knife (see page 3)

Aqua blue acrylic paint

Small paintbrush

Plastic ferns

Hot glue gun (see page 5)

Foil paper in several colors for sea creature decorations

Standard white craft glue (see page 6)

1 large and several small plastic pearl beads (optional)

1/2 yard short fringe

1 (2-ounce) package flesh-colored polymer clay

1 (2-inch-diameter) wooden bead

Toothpick

Glitter in a bold, sparkly color

Thin black marker

Doll hair

1 chenille stem (see page 3)

MAKES 1 TOILET PAPER COZY

INSTRUCTIONS

1. Measure 5^1/$_2$ inches from the bottom of the bleach bottle, and cut the bottle in half with a craft knife. Turn the bottom half of the bottle over, open-side down. This will be your cozy. Paint the outside of the cozy with the acrylic paint, and let it dry completely, about 1 hour.

2. Cut the plastic ferns into small pieces, and hot-glue them upright around the bottom of the cozy.

3. Cut small sea creature shapes from the foil paper, and use the standard white craft glue to attach them to the sides of the cozy. If you'd like, glue the large pearl bead to the top of the cozy and glue the small pearl beads around the sides as if they were bubbles. Hot-glue the fringe around the bottom, below the ferns.

4. To create the mermaid, form the polymer clay into the shape of a seated mermaid's body, such that she will rest atop the cozy. Form the neck to a size that will fit inside the hole in the wooden bead. Poke a hole with a toothpick on either side of the upper body where you will insert chenille stems for the mermaid's arms. When you are satisfied with your mermaid,

bake the figure in the oven according to the instructions on the clay package. Allow the figure to cool completely.

5. Using the paintbrush, apply craft glue all over the mermaid's body to cover from the waist down. Paint a bikini-shaped top with the glue and sprinkle glitter generously over the whole shape. Shake off the excess glitter and allow the glue to dry completely, about 1 hour.

6. Place a drop of craft glue inside the wooden bead and glue the bead to the mermaid's neck. Draw eyes and a mouth on the bead with the marker. Glue pieces of doll hair to the head and insert two pieces of chenille stem into the holes on either side of the body. Position the arms in a glamorous pose. Hot-glue the mermaid to the top of the cozy.

BRIDGE OR CANASTA PLACEMAT SET

FOR YOUR **BRIDGE** OR **CANASTA** GROUP
SHUFFLE OUT PLACEMATS AND COASTERS THAT FOLLOW SUIT!

ust out your knitting needles (and a crochet hook) to create this great placemat and coaster set with a playing card theme. You can either choose four different colors for the card suit motifs or use the traditional red and black. Note that you have to know how to knit and crochet to make this project. Whip up some mai tais, fill a cut-glass bowl with mixed nuts, and you're ready to play cards in style.

MATERIALS

4 skeins DK or light worsted-weight, machine-washable yarn (such as Lion Brand baby soft) for the main color

Size 6 (U.S.) knitting needles

1 skein of each contrasting color yarn for the card suit motifs

Size G crochet hook

Damp cloth for blocking

Straight pins

ABBREVIATIONS

beg = beginning

CC = contrasting color

k = knit

MC = main color

p = purl

sc = single crochet

st(s) = stitch(es)

MAKES 4 PLACEMENTS AND 4 COASTERS

INSTRUCTIONS FOR THE PLACEMATS

Gauge

4 sts = 1 inch; 5 rows = 1 inch

1. Using MC yarn, cast on 66 sts. Work in the following pattern (seed st) for 6 rows:

   Row 1: *K1, p1; repeat from * across. Row 2: *P1, k1; repeat from * across.

   This is the border pattern, to be used in the first 6 rows and the last 6 rows of each mat and in the 4 sts at the beg and end of every row.

2. Row 7: K1, p1, k1, p1, k58, k1, p1, k1, p1. Row 8: P1, k1, p1, k1, p58, p1, k1, p1, k1. Continue repeating these rows until the work measures 6 inches from the bottom of the work.

3. Next row: Still working 4 seed sts at the beginning and end of each row, start to follow the chart for one of the card suit motifs, using CC yarn. When changing from one color to another, always cross the new yarn over the old to avoid forming a hole. When the MC is left at the back of the work, twist it once around the working color every 3rd st to carry

it along the row, being careful to leave enough slack in the carried color to avoid crimping the card suit sts.

4. After completing the card suit motif, cut and fasten off the CC yarn, and continue in the MC for 2 more rows. Then work 6 rows of border sts, as in step 1 above, and bind off all sts.

5. To block the placemat, wet it completely with water and lay it on a towel on a flat surface. Pin the placemat to the towel in a flat, even shape and allow it to dry completely.

6. Repeat to make one placemat for each card suit.

INSTRUCTIONS FOR THE COASTERS

1. Using MC yarn, cast on 33 sts. Row 1: K all sts.

2. Row 2: P all sts.

3. Continue in stockinette st (k1 row, p1 row) for 4 more rows. Then begin to work the card suit motif in a CC following the chart.

4. Once you complete the motif, work 4 more rows in stockinette st, and then bind off all sts. To block the coaster, follow the instructions for blocking in step 5 above.

5. Repeat to make one coaster for each card suit.

Crocheted & Knitted Kitchen Craft: Lily Design Book No. 53 copyright © 1950 by Lily Mills Company.

CARD SUIT THROW PILLOWS

These novel scatter cushions ARE REAL ACES!

*T*hese charming card suit pillows are made of brightly colored felt. Rather than buying 9 by 12-inch sheets of craft felt, this project requires the felt that is sold by the yard in rolls 36 or 72 inches wide.

MATERIALS

4 (24-inch) paper squares

Pencil

Scissors

Straight pins

Felt (see page 4) in two colors, 4 yards per color from 36-inch rolls or 2 yards per color from 72-inch rolls

Black felt for the pillow gussets, 1 yard from a 36-inch role or $1/2$ yard from a 72-inch roll

Needle and thread

Sewing machine (optional; see page 6)

Loose pillow stuffing (see page 5)

8 button forms for making fabric-covered buttons, or 8 black buttons

MAKES 4 PILLOWS

INSTRUCTIONS

1. Fold one of the paper squares in half, and draw half of one of the card suit shapes on it, keeping the fold in the middle of the shape and making the half shape at least 15 inches long and $7^1/2$ inches wide (larger is fine, if you want bigger pillows). Cut the half shape out of both layers, and unfold the paper; this process ensures a symmetrical shape. Repeat this step for the three other suit shapes.

2. Pin each shape pattern to the color of felt you wish, and cut out the shape. Repeat to cut out a second set of shapes (one for the front and one for the back).

3. Cut the black felt into $1^1/2$-inch strips, and hand-sew them together end to end until they are long enough to wrap around the edge of each pillow shape to form a gusset. To join the ends of the felt strips together, simply place the right sides of two strips together and sew through both strips across the width about $1/4$ inch from the end. (A *gusset* is a piece of fabric added between other pieces to give shape to an item. In this project, the gusset is sewn onto the edges between the front and back shapes, to give the pillow depth.)

4. Pin the gusset strips between the back and front shapes of each pillow. Starting on a fairly straight part of the shape, stitch the gusset and the front together all around the pillow, keeping the stitching about $1/8$ inch away from the edge. Repeat for the gusset and the back, but stop about 3 inches from the beginning, to leave an opening. Stuff the pillow firmly with the loose stuffing, and then stitch the opening closed. Repeat for the other pillows.

5. If you are using fabric-covered buttons, pull the halves apart (if necessary), cut out circles of felt slightly larger than the button tops, tuck a circle around the top and edges of each button form, and snap on the back of the form, which holds the felt in place. Position one of the black or felt-covered buttons in the center of each pillow on the front and back sides. Then stitch the front button through the pillow tightly to the back button to create an indent on each side.

CROCHETED *Doll Face* FRIDGIES

CHERUBIC DOLLS *happily watch over your kitchen from the* **ICEBOX DOOR!**

*C*rochet yourself a wonderfully tacky little doll magnet to hang on your fridge—just make sure it doesn't scare your friends and family away! You can buy doll faces in the doll-making section of a craft supply store. If you have trouble finding them where you live, check out the Resource Guide (page 172) for some online sources. When you're working with kitschy doll faces, the cheaper and tackier the yarn, the better the project will look—a rare opportunity to go for the worst. Note that you need to know how to crochet to do this project.

MATERIALS

1 skein sport-weight yarn in main color

Size H crochet hook

1 skein sport-weight yarn in contrasting color

Tapestry needle

1 (3^1/$_2$-inch) doll face (available at craft supply stores)

Hot glue gun (see page 5)

1 magnet (available at craft supply stores and hardware stores)

ABBREVIATIONS

beg = beginning

CC = contrasting color

ch = chain

dc = double crochet

foll = following

MC = main color

rnd(s) = round(s)

sc = single crochet

sl st = slip stitch

sp(s) = space(s)

st(s) = stitch(es)

( ) = repeat steps within parentheses the number of times specified

MAKES 1 DOLL FACE MAGNET

INSTRUCTIONS

1. Foundation: With MC, ch 5, and join with sl st to form ring.

2. Rnd 1: Ch 3 (counts as 1 dc), make 23 dc into ring, sl st to top of ch-3 (24 dc total).

3. Rnd 2: Ch 3, 1 dc into same stitch, 2 dc in every st around, join with sl st to top of ch-3.

4. Rnd 3: Ch 3, 1 dc into same st (1 dc into next st, 2 dc in next st). Repeat around, join with sl st to top of ch-3.

5. Rnd 4: (Ch 5, skip 1 st, sc in next st, ch 3, skip next st, sc in next st). Repeat around.

6. Rnd 5: Working behind rnd 4 and off of rnd 3 (and keeping the front side of the piece facing you), sl st into first skipped st of rnd 3. (Ch 5, sc in next skipped st, ch 3, sc in next skipped st). Repeat around. Now you should have a double row of work, formed off of rnd 3. Rnd 4 is in the front, and rnd 5 is in the back. Fasten off.

7. Rnds 6 and 7: Join CC to center of ch-5 sp of rnd 4, ch 3 (counts as 1 dc), 4 dc into same ch-5 sp (1 sc into ch-3 sp, 5 dc into ch-5 sp). Repeat around twice. Fasten off.

8. Finishing: With MC, ch 80 to make a cord. Fasten off and leave a tail. Using the tapestry needle, weave ch-80 cord through loops of inside border. These are the loops created by rnd 4, which make the "inside" rnd, whereas rnd 5 makes the "outside" rnd. Make 2 pom-poms in MC and add them to the ends of the ch-80 cord. Now that the crocheting is done, weave in loose ends.

9. Place the doll face in the center of the bonnet, tighten the cord to secure the face, and tie a bow. Hot-glue a magnet onto the back, and stick your frilly doll face on the fridge.

Beaded FRUIT

You'll take a shine to these
BEADED BEAUTIES!

*B*eaded fruit dredges up memories of relatives who had these on their kitchen table. No need to pine for this artful relic of the past, because now you can create some of your very own. The number of beads, sequins, and pins you'll need will vary depending on the size of the fake fruit, but a good approximation is 300 beads and pins for each fruit. "Sequin pins" are what you use to attach the beads. These are miniature versions of traditional straight pins. All the supplies for this project should be readily available at a large craft supply store.

MATERIALS

About 300 translucent plastic beads per piece of fruit, in the colors of the fruit

About 300 sequin pins per piece of fruit

Enough pieces of plastic fruit, or Styrofoam fruit shapes, to fill your bowl

About 300 sequins per piece of fruit, in the colors of the beads (optional)

Thumb-size thimble (optional)

Decorative fruit bowl

MAKES 1 BOWL OF BEADED FRUIT

INSTRUCTIONS

1. String a bead on the pin and push the pin into the bottom of the piece of fruit. Working up from the bottom, repeat this step over and over until the piece of fruit is completely covered in beads and no surface of the fruit shows through. For even more sparkle, use sequins in addition to the beads. String a bead and then a sequin in a similar color on each pin before inserting it into the fruit. You may want to wear a thimble so your thumb doesn't get sore.

2. Repeat step 1 for as many pieces of fruit as your bowl will hold.

3. Place your bowl filled with fruit prominently in the middle of the kitchen table, and revel in the reactions of your guests. Hey, at least this fruit will never spoil!

MACARONI *Glamour* ACCESSORIES

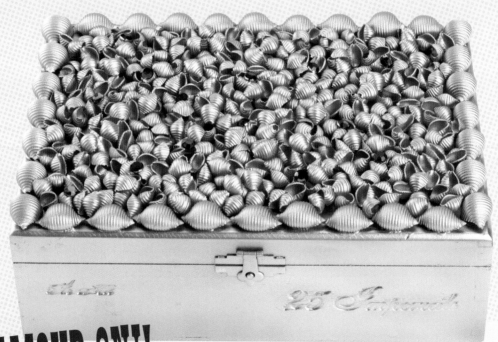

GLAMOUR-ONI!

Give an old cigar box new allure with macaroni!

*R*omantic tradition has it that Marco Polo brought pasta back with him to Italy in 1295 after 12 years of adventuring in Asia. For centuries, Italian kitchens simmered and stewed pasta to the highest peaks of culinary ecstasy. Some 650 years later, pasta took on new life—as an art form to be glued onto ordinary objects and painted gold. Dried pasta comes in all kinds of interesting shapes, and it's cheap. The possibilities for macaroni-adorned objets d'art are endless. Coordinate a gift set for a retro-loving friend, or bedeck all the objects in a room for an unforgettably kitschy look.

Mac and Gold Jewel Box

MATERIALS

Standard white craft glue (see page 6)

Dried pasta in various shapes

1 empty cardboard cigar box (see page 3)

Stack of newspapers

Gold spray paint (see page 6)

Small plastic pearls, beads, and other decorations

MAKES 1 JEWELRY BOX

INSTRUCTIONS

1. Glue various shapes of pasta to the top and sides of the cigar box in a symmetrical or free-form pattern.

2. When the glue has thoroughly dried, about 30 minutes, lay the box on the stack of newspapers, either outside or in a well-ventilated room, and spray it with the gold paint. You may have to spray one side at a time and let it dry according to the manufacturer's instructions before painting the next side.

3. After the paint has dried completely, add more sparkle and beauty by gluing on small plastic pearls, beads, and other decorations.

Glamour Tissue Box

Decorate an empty box of tissues, and cut out the bottom of the box so you can pop it over a new stack of tissues again and again.

Hand Mirror Magic

Give a worn-out hand mirror new life as a gift for that glamour-puss friend who has everything. Mask the mirror glass with a piece of adhesive contact paper. Then decorate and spray-paint the frame. When everything has dried completely, peel off the contact paper.

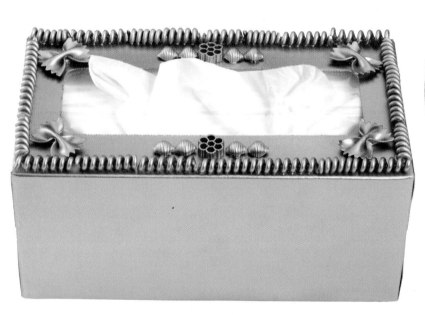

Gilded Coasters

For your next party, decorate cottage cheese or yogurt lids with a circle of glued-on macaroni. Spray-paint them gold and enjoy your tacky new coasters.

Picture of Elegance

Decorate and gild a plain unfinished wooden picture or wall mirror frame. First, remove the glass, backing, and other parts. Then glue on the macaroni, and spray-paint the frame. When it is dry, reassemble the parts.

Decorating with Macaroni copyright © 1964 by Aleene's, Inc.

DECOUPAGE LOVE-LETTER BOX

DON'T THROW
AWAY THAT
STURDY BOX!
USE DECOUPAGE
TO TURN IT INTO A
WORK OF ART!

*T*hemed keepsake boxes make great gifts (and gift boxes) for special occasions, such as baby showers and weddings. Find relevant imagery to paste onto your box from sheets of wrapping paper, wallpaper, old books or magazines, and comic books. You can even decoupage a box made of acid-free cardboard for photographs; it will protect your photos from the effects acids can have on paper over time. The love-themed box shown here is perfect for storing steamy love letters and keepsakes from hot dates.

MATERIALS

Acrylic paint and paintbrush

1 sturdy wooden or cardboard box with lid, heart-shaped if possible

Cut-out images from magazines, books, wallpaper, wrapping paper, or other sources

Small and medium sponge paintbrushes

Decoupage glue (see page 4)

MAKES 1 LOVE-LETTER BOX

INSTRUCTIONS

1. Paint the entire box a solid color, and let the paint dry thoroughly according to the manufacturer's instructions.

2. Arrange your cutouts on the box, working with one surface at a time. When you have the layout you want, use the small sponge paintbrush to apply a thin, even layer of decoupage glue on the back of each paper cutout, and gently apply the piece right side up to the box with your fingers. Smooth out any bubbles or wrinkles.

3. Once you have glued all the cutouts to the first side of the box, seal that side by brushing on a few coats of the decoupage glue with the medium sponge paintbrush. Allow the glue to dry completely between coats according to the manufacturer's instructions.

4. Follow steps 2 and 3 for the next side of the box, until all sides are decorated and sealed. To give the box a consistent sheen, also brush a coat of decoupage glue onto any side of the box without any cutouts on it.

CLOTHING

TERRY LOINCLOTHS

GAY TIMES WILL BE HAD BY ALL WITH THESE AFTER-SHOWER **TERRY COVER-UPS!**

I just had to include this project from my collection of vintage craft books because it was so preposterous—seemingly with no self-awareness of just how funny it is. Although it's faster to stitch these up by machine if you have a sewing machine and know how to use it, you can also do the job by hand with needle and thread. You'll need to know basic sewing techniques, such as hemming, threading a cord through a casing, and attaching a pocket.

MATERIALS

Measuring tape

Scissors

2 bath towels (approximately 40 by 60 inches or 28 by 54 inches)

Sewing machine (optional; see page 6), or needle and thread

1 yard heavy cord (for loincloth)

1 yard bias tape or ribbon (for wraparound)

MAKES 1 LOINCLOTH AND 1 WRAPAROUND

INSTRUCTIONS FOR THE LOINCLOTH

1. Measure and cut a bath towel to 37 by 18 inches, slightly curving the long sides in toward the middle (see figure A on page 110).

2. Machine- or hand-stitch a $1/2$-inch hem on the long (curved) sides. Then make a 1-inch hem on the top and bottom (short) edges, to serve as a casing.

3. Fold the towel in half so that the top and bottom edges meet. Thread the cord through the 1-inch hems, and tie the loincloth at one side of the waist.

4. Cut a 3 by 6-inch pocket (see figure A) from a leftover piece of towel. Stitch a hem on all sides of the pocket, and then sew it onto the front of the loincloth as shown in the diagram.

INSTRUCTIONS FOR THE WRAPAROUND

1. Measure and cut a bath towel to 54 by 18 inches. Stitch a hem around all four edges of the towel. (If your bath towel is roughly 54 by 18 inches already, just use it as is, with no cutting or hemming.)

2. Cut a 5 by 4-inch five-sided pocket (with a point at the bottom) from a leftover piece of towel. Stitch a hem on all sides of the pocket, and then sew it onto one side of the towel at a jaunty angle (see figure B).

3. Cut the bias tape in half, hem one end of each piece, and sew the other ends to the top corners of the towel (see figure B) to tie the towel at the side after wrapping it around the waist.

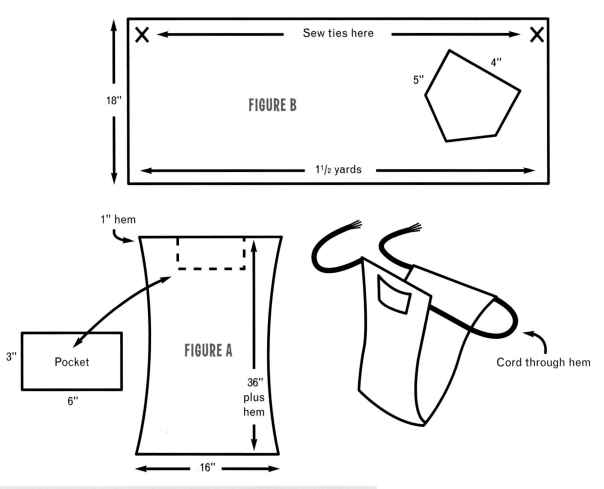

Sew ties here

18"

FIGURE B

5"   4"

1½ yards

1" hem

3"   Pocket   6"

FIGURE A

36" plus hem

16"

Cord through hem

Make It with Curtains and Terry Cloth copyright © 1965 by Graff Publications, Inc.

TOTE BAG APRON

FIRST IT'S AN **APRON,** THEN IT'S A **TOTE BAG!**

The top of this apron disappears into the front to form a drawstring bag, which stores your knitting, embroidery, or whatever you're working on. As an apron, it keeps everything you need in your lap—nothing will roll out onto the floor. As a bag, it's handy for bringing your current craft project with you anywhere you go. Note that, for this project you need to have some experience with your sewing machine or sewing by hand. Specifically, you should know how to hem, gather, topstitch, sew casings, and sew pockets. A book on the basics of sewing will teach you how to do these things.

MATERIALS

Measuring tape or ruler

Scissors

1 yard (45-inch-wide) cotton fabric (plain or patterned)

Sewing machine (optional; see page 6), or needle and thread

Iron and ironing board

Straight pins

1^1/$_3$ yards baby rickrack (optional)

2^1/$_2$ yards (^{1}/$_4$-inch-wide) black rayon cord or bias tape

MAKES 1 APRON

	36"		3"
			3"
7^1/$_2$"	Apron Top	Waistband	3"
		13"	
	Back Pocket	Front Pocket	22^1/$_2$"
	18"	18"	

INSTRUCTIONS

1. Measure and cut out the fabric pieces according to the diagram.

2. To make the front pocket, fold the right sides of the pocket fabric together crosswise, leaving one side 3 inches longer than other. Stitch the sides together, leaving a ^{1}/$_2$-inch seam allowance. Turn the fabric right side out, and press.

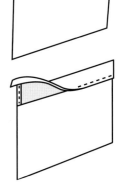

Wrong side of fabric

3. Turn the sides of the 3-inch flap under ^{1}/$_4$ inch toward the wrong side two times, and hem them. Fold the top edge down ^{1}/$_4$ inch, and press it.

4. Fold the flap in half to meet the top of the pocket, and stitch. To make a casing for the drawstring, stitch across the flap

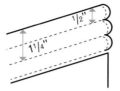

1/2 inch from the top fold and again 1 1/4 inches from the top.

5. Repeat steps 2–3 to make the back pocket.

6. Hem the sides of the apron top by making a double turn of 1/4 inch toward the wrong side and stitching.

7. To attach the apron top to the back pocket, lay the apron top along the raw edge of the pocket and pin. Fold the pocket flap in half to cover the edges of the apron top and pocket. Pin, and stitch.

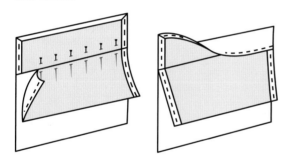

8. Make a casing in the flap for the back piece of the pocket by following step 4.

9. Lay the finished front pocket on the finished back pocket, and topstitch through all layers, starting at the bottom edge of the casing on one side, down the side, across the bottom, and up the other side just to the casing (be sure to leave the casing ends open, so the cord

can be inserted). Decorate the side and bottom edges with the baby rickrack.

10. Gather the raw edge of the apron top to 12 inches wide.

11. Lay the right side of the waistband on the wrong side of the gathered apron top; stitch them together 1/2 inch from the edge.

12. Stitch a 1/4-inch hem on both long sides and one short end of each of the apron ties.

13. Fold the waistband over to the right side of the apron top; turn the raw edge of the waistband under 1/4 inch. Fold the raw ends of the waistband inside 1/4 inch. Press these edges with an iron. Insert about 1/2 inch of the raw ends of the ties at either side of the waistband. Pin everything in place, and topstitch the waistband to the apron top and ties.

14. Cut the rayon cord in half. With the front pocket of the apron facing you, thread one piece of cord from the left side into the front pocket casing; continue around through the back pocket casing, and knot the two ends of the cord at the left side. Insert the second cord from the right side into the front casing, continue around through the back casing, and knot the ends at the right side.

NOVEL NECKTIE APRON

HE WEARS A NECKTIE TO HIS JOB; NOW YOU CAN WEAR ONE IN THE KITCHEN!

*T*his funky apron is a great way to use a collection of hopelessly out-of-date neckties. It requires some basic knowledge of how to use a sewing machine, if you want to make quick work of it, but you can sew it by hand in leisurely fashion, too. Note that you'll need to know how to make zigzag stitches by machine or by hand.

MATERIALS

Iron and ironing board

8 neckties (or more for a wider apron)

Measuring tape

Scissors

Sewing machine (optional; see page 6), or needle and thread

Straight pins

1 yard pom-pom fringe

MAKES 1 APRON

INSTRUCTIONS

1. Iron the neckties to smooth them out.

2. Measure 17 inches from the bottom tip of the wide part of at least 6 ties, and cut across the width at that point.

3. Lay the wide pieces side by side on a surface, arranging them in the order in which you are going to sew them together. Using the zigzag stitch on your sewing machine or with a needle and thread, sew one tie to another along the long edges.

4. To create the waistband, measure the width of the top of the apron. Use the skinny end of one of the ties you've already used to match this measurement. Position the piece along the top edge of the apron, overlapping $1/4$ inch. Pin the waistband to the apron and then sew the pieces together using a straight stitch. Using the two remaining neckties, sew the skinny ends of each tie to either end of the waistband to form a long tie that wraps around the waist and ties into a large bow.

5. Sew the pom-pom fringe to the pointy bottom edge of the apron with a straight stitch (see resources section) for the perfect kitschy touch.

HEADBANDS
for All Occasions

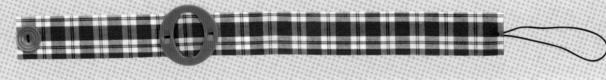

It can be windy in your *dreamboat's convertible,* so you'd better keep every hair in place!

*H*ere's a really simple technique for creating a stylish ribbon headband. It stretches to fit any size head because the elastic at one end hooks around the button on the other end. Ribbon can be found in so many styles that you can make a headband to go with every outfit. Or use plain ribbon, and decorate it with buttons, sequins, buckles, embroidery, fake flowers, pom-poms—you name it!

MATERIALS

16 inches ribbon

Anti-fray solution (available at craft or sewing supply stores), if needed

Iron and ironing board

Needle and thread

8 inches thin elastic cord (available at craft or sewing supply stores)

1 button

MAKES 1 HEADBAND

INSTRUCTIONS

1. To make sure the ends of the ribbon don't unravel, apply the anti-fray solution to them, or hem the ends by folding them under, pressing with an iron, and sewing them.

2. To form a loop with the elastic, fold it in half, and sew both ends to one end of the ribbon. Sew the button to the other end of the ribbon. Put the ribbon on your head, and loop the elastic around the button under your hair at the back.

LOOM-KNIT SCARF

KNIT A LOVELY STOLE

EVEN IF YOU DON'T KNOW A KNIT FROM A PURL!

Weaving on a slot loom is actually a type of simplified knitting that quickly produces a pretty ribbed knit. You can make scarves, headbands, table runners, and other rectangular items easily using this method. Try creating several straight strips and sewing them together to make more complicated items. If you don't have access to a saw, have pieces of wood cut to size at your local building supply store or lumberyard.

MATERIALS

Sandpaper

2 (2 x 12 x 1¹/₂-inch) wood boards

2 (2 x 5 x 1¹/₂-inch) wood boards

Hammer

50 brads (also called 18-gauge nails)

4 (2-inch) nails

1 skein (200 grams) worsted-weight yarn

Knitting needle, or darning needle (a thick sewing needle)

Crochet hook

Scissors

MAKES 1 LOOM AND 1 SCARF

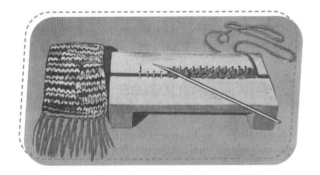

INSTRUCTIONS FOR THE LOOM

1. To make the loom, sand all four wood boards until smooth, so that the yarn won't snag when you use the loom.

2. Hammer an even row of brads ¹/₂ inch apart and ¹/₈ inch from the edge along one long side of each 12-inch board, leaving enough of each nail sticking up so that two thicknesses of your yarn can fit on it easily without slipping off. (Each whole row of brads should be just slightly wider than you'd like your finished weaving to be.)

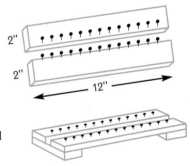

3. Place the short boards 12 inches apart, and lay the long boards across them, leaving a ¹/₂-inch-wide space between the long boards. Using the 2-inch-long nails, nail the long boards to the short boards at the edges.

INSTRUCTIONS FOR A ONE-COLOR SCARF

1. To thread the loom, position it horizontally in front of you. Starting at the left, knot the end of the yarn around the leftmost brad of the board farther from you. (This first knot eventually gets treated like any other loop.) Then loop the yarn clockwise around the leftmost brad on the closer board (the yarn will cross over itself as you loop). Be sure not to thread the yarn tautly; keep it relaxed. Next, loop the yarn counterclockwise around the next empty brad on the farther board.

Continue in this way, looping around brads on opposite boards until you have looped the rightmost brads.

2. To weave the second row, work the yarn back across the loom from right to left on top of the first loops but in a simpler manner. As shown in the diagram, simply run the yarn around the back of each brad and then across to the brad on the opposite board and around its back. Do this until you reach the left end of the loom (the yarn will *not* cross over itself for this row).

3. Since you just worked from the right to the left, you'll go from left to right in this step. With the knitting or darning needle, lift the lower loop on each brad over the upper loop and off the brad. Continue lifting loops over and off this way down one side of the loom and then back across the other side. The end brad used for turning directions has only one loop, so it can be woven only on alternate rows.

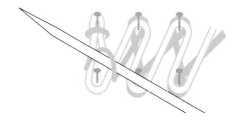

4. Now, wind yarn around all the brads again, from left to right this time, as you did for the second row, around the back of each brad, across to the opposite brad, around its back, across to next brad opposite, and so on, making each loop on top of the loop remaining on each brad. Bring the bottom loops over the top loops as described above. Repeat this process until the woven strip is the length you want your scarf to be.

5. To finish your work with a nice tight edge, use a crochet hook. Insert the hook through the loops on the last two brads as shown in the diagram. Pull loop 2 through loop 1. You should now have one loop on your crochet hook. Repeat this step for the next two loops on the next two brads; note that since there was already one loop on your crochet hook, you'll now be pulling loop 2 through two loops. Repeat this step until you reach the opposite side of the scarf. You'll be left with an even edge and one loose loop at the end. Thread the tail end of the yarn through this loop and pull lightly. Weave the end of the yarn back into the scarf.

Remove first two loops

Pull 2 through 1

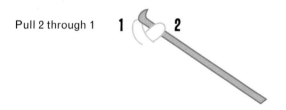

6. To make a fringe, cut pieces of yarn about 6 inches long and fold each in half. Loop the yarn through an end stitch of the scarf, tuck the ends through the loop as shown, and pull tight. Repeat at regular intervals along the ends of the scarf.

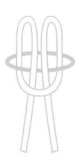

INSTRUCTIONS FOR A STRIPED SCARF

To make stripes, buy half the amount of yarn in each color. Thread the loom, and weave two rows with the first color. Then tie on the second color, without cutting the first yarn, and weave two rows in the second color. Pick up the first yarn, and weave the next two rows; pick up the second color, and continue in this fashion to the desired length. Make the fringe by alternating the two colors, if you wish.

Tailored DICKEY

A welcome invention for busy **CAREER GIRLS—** saves on laundry and dresses up the plainest sweater!

A dickey is a small false shirt front (about the size of a bib) to wear under a sweater as if you had a whole shirt on underneath. Dickeys can be made of any fabric you'd like, but, if you're a beginner at sewing, 100 percent cotton is the easiest to work with. As a rule, slippery or stretchy fabrics are more difficult to sew. Try using a funky cotton print that will make a statement peeking out from under your sweater. Note that the instructions for this project require some basic experience with the techniques used in sewing clothing, including trimming seams, clipping corners, and whipstitching.

MATERIALS

1 yard fabric of your choice

Measuring tape or ruler

Scissors

Sewing machine (optional; see page 6)

Needle and thread

Iron and ironing board

MAKES 1 DICKEY

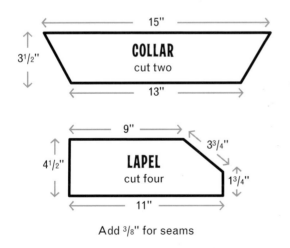

Add 3/8" for seams

INSTRUCTIONS

1. Fold the fabric in half, so you can cut two pieces at once. Using the dimensions shown on the pattern, but adding on 3/8 inch all the way around for the seams, cut two pieces for the collar and four for the lapels.

2. Place the collar pieces right sides together, and sew around three sides, 3/8 inch from the edge, leaving the neck edge open. Trim the seams, and clip the corners. Turn the collar right side out, and press with the iron to make the corners crisp.

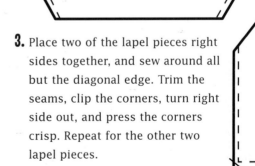

3. Place two of the lapel pieces right sides together, and sew around all but the diagonal edge. Trim the seams, clip the corners, turn right side out, and press the corners crisp. Repeat for the other two lapel pieces.

4. Place the diagonal edge of one lapel along the neck edge at one end of the collar, and sew the lapel to only the top piece of the collar $3/8$ inch from the raw edges. Repeat for the other lapel at the other end of the collar. Turn the lapel seams to the inside of the collar, fold under the unsewn edge of the collar $3/8$ inch, and whipstitch (see resources section) the unsewn edge to the lapels at the ends and to the front of the collar in the middle. Press.

5. To put on the dickey, hold it at points A and B, lift it over your head, and fit the collar across the back of your neck and around under your chin. Then straighten the lapels. Throw on your favorite sweater, pull out the collar of your fabulous new dickey, and you'll no longer be a Plain Jane!

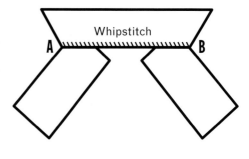

Whipstitch

A   B

TEMPTRESS COLLAR

ADD A TOUCH OF
PINUP-GIRL PIZZAZZ
TO A HUMDRUM COAT
OR SWEATER!

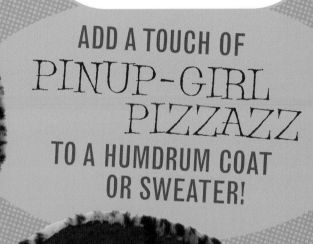

*T*his kicky collar will add a splash of 1950s bad girl flair. After you master the collar, you can experiment with other matching accents like cuffs or a headband made with the same fur. Fabric stores often carry a wide range of faux furs, so choose a fun leopard print or get even wilder with long and fluffy hot pink fur. For this project, you'll need a basic knowledge of how to sew clothing, including transfering markings from a pattern to fabric, trimming edges of seams, clipping curves, and whipstitching.

MATERIALS

Photocopier

Scissors

Pencil

1 yard faux fur

1 yard satin fabric

Sewing machine (optional; see page 6)

Needle and thread

24 inches (1/4-inch-wide) ribbon

Straight pins

Pencil, or other pointed tool, for pushing out corners and curves

Iron and ironing board

MAKES 1 COLLAR

INSTRUCTIONS

1. Enlarge the template to 150 percent on the photocopier. Cut out the pattern, and trace it on the wrong side of the fur and satin. Transfer all markings onto the fur and satin as well. Cut one piece from each fabric.

2. First you'll create a "dart" (a sewn fold that gives fabric shape) at the part of the collar that rests behind your neck. Fold the fur piece in half with the right sides together, and machine- or hand-stitch a 3/8-inch seam along the dotted lines (see template). Unfold the halves, and trim the edges of the fold.

3. Cut the ribbon in half. Hem one end of each ribbon. Pin the unhemmed ends to each end of the collar at the neck edge, following the Xs marked in the diagram; you need to lay each ribbon facing inward, right side down against the right side of the collar, and leave 1/2 inch of ribbon overhanging the end of the collar. Tie the hemmed ends of the ribbons together in a bow to keep them in the middle of the collar (away from the edges), so you can avoid sewing over them in step 4.

4. With right sides together, pin the faux fur to the satin collar piece, and sew a $3/8$-inch seam all around except for a 4-inch opening on a fairly flat area. Trim the seam, and clip the curves.

5. Remove the pins, and turn the collar right side out through the opening, releasing the ends of the ribbons from their bow. Using a pencil or other pointed tool, poke out the curves.

6. To close the opening, fold the raw edges in $3/8$ inch, and whipstitch (see resources section) the opening closed. Fluff out the fur to hide the stitches.

7. Iron the satin side of the collar flat for a nice finish. Now, tie it around your neck, and pray for snow!

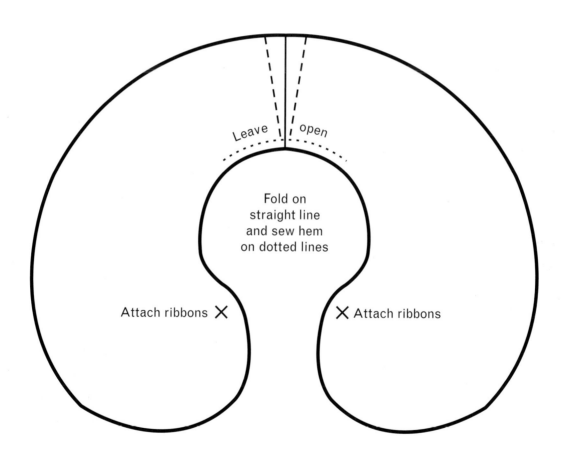

Leave open

Fold on
straight line
and sew hem
on dotted lines

Attach ribbons ✕

✕ Attach ribbons

NOVELTIES

RECYCLED RECORD COVERS

CREATE NEAT-O NOTEBOOKS AND NOVELTIES FROM RAD PLATTER COVERS!

*E*ver seen an old record cover that was just too cool to throw away even though the record was totally unplayable? You learned about all the amazing things you could make with the record itself (see pages 46–51); now see what you can do with the record cover. The notebook is refillable, the note holder has a handy hanger, and the file folders are thrifty, plus they all look fabulous.

MATERIALS

Old record covers

Cutting mat (see page 4)

Metal ruler

Craft knife (see page 3)

For the Notebook

100 sheets (8¹/₂ by 11-inch) 3-hole-punched paper, or more as desired

Hole punch

Scissors, if needed

1 yard ribbon, or 6 metal eyelets and an eyelet-setting tool (available at craft supply stores), or 3 book rings (available at office supply stores), or 3 screw posts and 24 inches of bookbinding tape (available at craft supply stores)

For the Note Holder

1 picture hanger

For the File Folders

Standard white craft glue (see page 6)

1 index tab for each folder

MAKES 1 NOTEBOOK/SCRAPBOOK, 1 NOTE HOLDER, AND 1 OR MORE FILE FOLDERS

INSTRUCTIONS FOR THE NOTEBOOK

1. Place your record cover on the cutting mat. Use the metal ruler and craft knife to cut the front and back of the cover into two rectangles just slightly larger than your paper. (If you are using standard 8¹/₂ by 11-inch paper, then cut the cover to 9 by 11¹/₂ inches.) The front of the record cover will be the front cover of the notebook, and the back of the record cover will be the back of the notebook.

2. Using the punched paper as a guide, punch holes through the back edges of the notebook covers. Stack the pieces to assemble the notebook: back cover (outside down), 3-hole paper, front cover (outside up). Then line up the holes.

3. Cut the ribbon into three 6-inch lengths. Thread each piece of ribbon through one set of holes, and tie its ends into a bow, leaving a bit of slack so the notebook will open and close easily. Alternatively, put the metal eyelets into the holes of the covers for a more polished look, and then thread the ribbon through them; or use the book rings that snap open and closed; or use the screw posts. Unlike book rings or ribbon, which allow the front cover to open freely, screw posts fight to keep it closed, so you need to make the front cover bendable: cut off a 1-inch lengthwise strip at the left side of the cover, including the holes. Then, using the bookbinding tape on the inside and outside of the cover, reattach the strip just a few millimeters away from where it was. This creates a small gap that acts as a joint where the front cover can bend.

INSTRUCTIONS FOR THE NOTE HOLDER

1. Place the record cover on the cutting mat so that the front is facing you and the opening is at the top. With the craft knife, slit down each side of the album cover, stopping about 4 inches from the bottom. Then cut across the front only (leaving the back of the album cover full length) to form a pocket that's the width of the album cover and 4 inches high. Use the craft knife to shape the back panel decoratively, as shown.

2. Attach a picture hanger to the outside of the back panel, and hang the note holder on the wall.

INSTRUCTIONS FOR THE FILE FOLDERS

1. Because album covers are slightly larger than 12 by 12 inches, they are ideal for storing standard-size notebook paper. With the front of the record cover facing you and the opening at the top, use a craft knife to slit all the way down the two sides to create a folder.

2. Glue one of the index tabs to the top of each folder. Stagger the tabs horizontally.

3. Repeat for as many file folders as you wish.

PLAYING-CARD *Notebooks*

SHOW YOUR CARDS!

These little notebooks are bound along one edge using standard white craft glue, so the effect is similar to that of a typical memo pad with a gummy binding along one side. If you want to make lots of notebooks, cutting paper to size can be time consuming. A heavy-duty paper cutter makes the job go much faster. Or go to your local copy shop to have the paper cut to whatever size you want. It usually costs only a few dollars. With this technique you can create an endless supply of small gifts that are perfect for the card-loving guys and gals in your life. Personalize each notebook by choosing a card for the cover that has special meaning, such as a friend's lucky number.

MATERIALS

Measuring tape or ruler

1 playing card

Scissors

10 sheets plain white copy paper

1 piece cardboard

Newspaper

1 clamp, or a heavy object to weight down the notebook

Standard white craft glue (see page 6)

3 inches ($5/8$-inch-wide) ribbon

MAKES 1 NOTEBOOK

INSTRUCTIONS

1. Measure your playing card, and cut 40 rectangles of copy paper to size. (Playing cards are usually 2 by 3 inches, but measure yours to make sure.) If your playing cards have rounded corners, the paper will stick out a bit at the corners; this is okay.

2. Cut the piece of cardboard to the same size as the playing card.

3. Spread out the newspaper to protect your work surface. Assemble the notebook with the cardboard at the bottom, your desired number of paper pages in the middle, and the playing card on top. Line up all the pieces, and clamp them together from the right edge or put the heavy object on top of them to hold them together.

4. Apply a thick layer of glue along the left edge to bind the pieces together. The clamp helps keep the pages together as the glue sets (about

15 minutes). Apply two or three more layers of glue at intervals of 15 minutes or so.

5. When the glue on the binding has dried completely, cut a piece of ribbon the same height as the notebook. Apply a thin, even layer of glue all over the back of the ribbon. Smooth the ribbon onto the glued edge of the notebook and over the front and back edges, for decoration and to hold the cover on more securely. When the ribbon is dry, the notebook is ready to use.

WHAT CAN YOU DO WITH A DECK THAT'S MISSING A FEW?

CREATE SMALL NOTEBOOKS FOR KEEPING BRIDGE SCORES!

FOIL ANIMALS

These projects came from a 1959 book called *Alcoa's Book of Decorations*, published by the Aluminum Company of America (of course). It's one of my favorite vintage craft books because each project is even more campy than the last one. You may be able to find this book on the Internet through used-book and auction sites, and, if you do, it's well worth it. Aren't you dying to learn how to make a tinfoil porcupine into which you stick toothpicks with cocktail wienies on them? Much to my dismay, the photo of that cocktail wienie porcupine was too small to reproduce legibly in this book. Otherwise, you can bet I would have included it.

MATERIALS

Plastic drinking straws, or disposable wooden chopsticks (available at Asian restaurant supply stores or Asian supermarkets)

5 small ($2^1/_2$-inch-diameter) and 4 medium ($3^1/_2$-inch diameter) Styrofoam balls

Scissors

Aluminum foil

Chenille stems (see page 3)

Black construction paper, or craft felt (see page 4)

Standard white craft glue (see page 6)

Craft knife (see page 3)

MAKES 1 BIRD, 1 BEAR, 1 GIRAFFE, AND 1 CAMEL

YOU CAN MAKE A MAGICAL MENAGERIE OF SPARKLY FRIENDS!

INSTRUCTIONS FOR THE BIRD

1. To make the bird's legs, insert two drinking straws close together into the bottom of a small Styrofoam ball (the bird's body). Cut the straws to the length you wish.

2. To make the neck, insert another straw into the top of the body; cut the straw to the length you wish. Insert the top of the straw (the neck) into another small Styrofoam ball for the head. Cover the entire figure with foil.

3. Mold feet of crushed foil, leaving an excess to attach them to the ends of the legs.

4. Use the chenille stems to construct a tail, beak, and wings, sticking them into the foil and Styrofoam. Cut eyes out of the construction paper or felt, and glue them onto the head.

INSTRUCTIONS FOR THE BEAR

1. Place one medium Styrofoam ball on top of another. Cover both balls with foil.

2. Add more foil to the top ball, and mold it into a bear face. Crush foil into arm and leg shapes, position them on the body, and cover everything with more foil to hold the pieces in place.

3. Form ears from crushed foil. With the craft knife, make indentations in either side of the Styrofoam ball head, and then insert the edges of the ears.

4. Make facial features from the construction paper or felt, and glue them onto the head.

INSTRUCTIONS FOR THE GIRAFFE

1. Use two small Styrofoam balls for the head and one medium Styrofoam ball for the body of the giraffe. Using a sheet of foil about 24 inches long, wrap one end around the two smaller balls to form the head. Bring the remaining foil down, crush some for a neck, and wrap the remainder around the medium ball for the body.

2. Add more foil to the body to make it thicker. Stick four straws into the body to form legs. Add more foil to the body, covering the legs to secure them.

3. Mold foil onto the head to form ears and horns. Make facial features from the construction paper or felt, and glue them onto the head. Cut spots from felt and glue them to the body.

INSTRUCTIONS FOR THE CAMEL

1. Cover a small Styrofoam ball with one end of a 24-inch length of foil, and mold it into a camel-shaped head (see photo).

2. Bring the remaining foil down, and crush some to form the neck. Use the rest to cover a medium Styrofoam ball for the body. Add more foil to form the hump. Crush two 8-inch-long pieces of foil into long, thin shapes, and drape them over the top of the body so that each forms two legs. Add more foil to hold the legs secure and to fill out the body shape.

3. Make facial features from the construction paper or felt, and glue them onto the head.

Merry Monsters

KOOKY
SPOOKY
Merry Monsters
ARE A
SCREAM!

I hate to admit this, but when I was kid, in the 1970s, my mom made me one of these, and
it scared the bejesus out of me. I kept it buried under my stuffed animals and out of sight
at all times. I had forgotten all about this creature until I stumbled on a stack of old craft
leaflets from the fifties, and there was "that scary yarn octopus thing." At least this incarnation
of the pattern admits that the little guys are monsters. My mom tried to pass it off as a cuddly,
lovable octopus. I wasn't buying.

MATERIALS

Light- or medium-weight yarn (2 skeins in one color for
Baby Oscar, 2 skeins of different colors for each of
Annabella and Oliver, and 4 skeins of one color for
Madam Pompadour)

3 strips of cardboard (4 by 13 inches for Baby Oscar,
4 by 19 inches for Annabella and Oliver, and 4 by 34 inches
for Madam Pompadour)

Scissors

Styrofoam balls for the head (3 inches in diameter for
Baby Oscar, 4 inches in diameter for Annabella and
Oliver, 5 inches in diameter for Madam Pompadour),
or loose pillow stuffing (see page 5)

Scraps of felt for eyes and mouths (see page 4)

Standard white craft glue (see page 6)

2 yards (³/₄-inch-wide) ribbon (for Madam Pompadour)

8 small bells (for Madam Pompadour)

MAKES 4 OCTOPUS MONSTERS

Merry Monsters copyright © 1962 Coats & Clark, Inc.

INSTRUCTIONS FOR BABY OSCAR

1. Wind the yarn 60 times around the 13-inch-
long cardboard. Leave a 1-yard tail of yarn
unwrapped. Slide the yarn loops off the cardboard and hold the yarn together so you have
a 13-inch-long bunch of yarn loops.

2. Grasp the long tail end of yarn, wrap it a few
times around the bunch of yarn 3 inches down
from the top, and tie it tightly. Now you'll have
two segments of yarn loops, one 3 inches long
and one 10 inches long.

3. Insert a pair of scissors into the very top of the
3-inch segment, and snip through all the
strands of yarn. (This forms the tuft of hair at
the top of Baby Oscar's head.)

4. Insert the scissors at the very bottom of the
10-inch segment of yarn and snip through all
the strands of yarn. Now the yarn is hanging
loose rather than in loops. This yarn will cover
the "head" and be braided into "legs."

5. Place one of the Styrofoam balls directly under
the 3-inch segment, and drape the loose 10-inch
strands around it to cover. Tightly grasp all the

long pieces of yarn right under the Styrofoam ball, loop the tail end of the yarn a few times around the dangling pieces under the head, and tie it tightly. From top to bottom you should have the tuft of hair, the covered Styrofoam head, and long loose pieces of yarn. (For a softer toy, use an equivalent-size ball of pillow stuffing for the head rather than a Styrofoam ball.)

6. Cut the tail end of the yarn so that it dangles to the same length as the rest of the dangling yarn.

7. Divide the dangling yarn into 11 sections of 11 strands. Further divide the 11 strands into three sections of 3, 4, and 4 strands and braid to form a leg. Tie a piece of yarn around the bottom of each braided leg to secure it, and trim the ends evenly.

8. Cut felt for the eyes and mouth, and glue them to the face.

INSTRUCTIONS FOR ANNABELLA AND OLIVER

Annabella and Oliver are made just like Baby Oscar except that you need 1 skein each of two different colors of yarn for each monster, and the 19-inch-long cardboard. Wrap one color of yarn 30 times around the cardboard (don't leave a long tail), and next to that wrap the second color 30 times (and do leave a 1-yard tail). Follow steps 1 through 8 above, keeping the two colors of yarn bunched together as shown in the photo. Make some braids using both colors, and use the contrasting yarn to tie the ends of the one-color braids.

INSTRUCTIONS FOR MADAM POMPADOUR

Using 4 skeins of yarn and the 34-inch-long cardboard, follow steps 1 and 2 for Baby Oscar above, wrapping the yarn 60 times. Tie off a 2-inch segment at the top, and leave the yarn at the top looped to look like a pompadour. Follow steps 4 through 8 to create Madam Pompadour's head and legs, but trim the tail close to the knot under the head so you can divide the leg yarn into 8 sections of 15 strands rather than 11 sections of 11 strands. Braid the legs using three groups of 5 strands each.

With the ribbon, tie a bow around the neck; then tie a bell onto the bottom of each leg.

From left: Annabella, Madam Pompadour, Baby Oscar, and Oliver

Plastic Bottle PIGGY BANK

SAVING UP
FOR A NEW
DECODER RING
OR A
HULA HOOP?

*W*hat could be thriftier than stashing your pennies in a piggy bank made from an empty bleach bottle? After trying this project, you may find yourself bleaching your whites more than usual to collect empty bottles. Or try cajoling your friends to save their bottles for you.

MATERIALS

Craft knife (see page 3)

1 empty plastic bleach bottle

1 (6 by 2-inch-diameter) white Styrofoam pole (available at craft supply stores)

4 sheets (9 by 12-inch) craft felt in black, orange, pink, and yellow (see page 4)

Hot glue gun (see page 5)

Thick white craft glue (see page 7)

Pencil

Paper

Scissors

2 (20-milimeter-diameter) movable eyes (available at craft supply stores)

Sequins or plastic gems

1 chenille stem (see page 3)

1 yard (¹/₂-inch-wide) ribbon

MAKES 1 PIGGY BANK

INSTRUCTIONS

1. Using the craft knife, cut a rectangular coin slot (large enough to fit a half-dollar) lengthwise in the side of the bottle about 1 inch below the handle. This will be the top of the piggy bank.

2. To make the legs, cut the Styrofoam cylinder into four 1¹/₂-inch-long pieces. Use the craft knife to shave a slant into one end of each piece so it will rest snugly against the curve of the bottle. Cut a piece of pink felt into 4 (1¹/₂ by 5-inch) rectangles and hot-glue one to each leg. Allow the glue to dry completely and trim away any excess felt. Using the craft glue, attach the four legs to the bottom of the bank.

3. Trace the patterns for the eyelashes, ears, and flowers (see page 144) onto the paper. Carefully cut them out with the scissors, and use them as stencils to mark and cut pieces from felt. Cut two eyelashes from the black felt, two ears from the pink felt, and flowers plus some polka dots (circles of various sizes) from the other colors of felt.

4. Glue one movable eye onto the round area of each felt eyelash, and then glue the eyelashes to the bottle on either side of the handle.

5. Cut a small slit in the bottom of each felt ear as shown on the pattern. Overlap the pieces on either side of the slit and glue them together to pucker the ear slightly in the center (this makes the ear stand up when you glue it to the bottle). Glue the ears 1¹/₂ inches apart on top of the head and between the handle and the coin slot

6. To make the nose, unscrew the bottle cap, and trace a circle around it on a piece of pink felt. Cut out the circle, and glue it onto the outside of the cap. Screw the cap back onto the bottle. Glue two sequins or two small circles of black felt onto the pink felt for nostrils. Measure and cut a ³/₄ by 6-inch strip of black felt to glue around the sides of the bottle cap.

7. Cut a 3 by 4-inch piece of orange felt for the blanket, and glue it to the top of the piggy bank, over the coin slot. Then cut a slit in the blanket to match the coin slot.

8. To make the tail, curl the chenille stem into a spiral and hot-glue it to the back of the piggy bank. Cut a 6-inch length of the ribbon, and tie a small bow around the tail.

9. Make a bow from the remaining ribbon, and glue it to the top of the pig's head between the ears. Glue the felt flowers, polka dots, and sequins or plastic gems decoratively onto the bottle, and allow everything to dry completely.

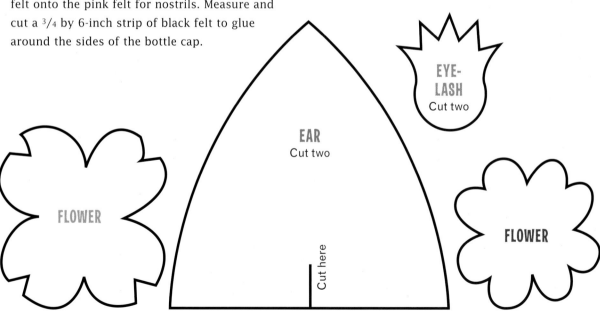

FLOWER

EAR
Cut two

EYE-LASH
Cut two

Cut here

FLOWER

LOCKER *or* OVER-THE-DOOR CADDIE

It's KEEN to keep your locker CLEAN!

*T*ake a load off the top shelf of a school locker with this caddie, or hang one over the back of any door in your house. It will hold everything from hair spray to shoes to your current knitting project in style, and it lets you see and grab your stuff in a flash. Note that you have to know how to sew hems, casings, box pleats, pockets, topstitching, and backstitching, either with a sewing machine or by hand, to make the caddie.

MATERIALS

Measuring tape

Scissors

$1^1/_2$ yards cotton fabric for the backing

Sewing machine (optional; see page 6), or needle and thread

Iron and ironing board

2 eyelets and an eyelet-setting tool (available at sewing supply stores)

$^1/_2$ yard cotton fabric for the large pleated pocket

$^1/_2$ yard cotton fabric for the medium-size pockets

Ribbon, iron-on letters, or rickrack for trimming pockets (optional)

$^1/_2$ yard cotton fabric for the small pockets

Wire cutters

1 wire coat hanger

Bright-colored heavyweight yarn or cord

Pliers

MAKES 1 CADDIE

INSTRUCTIONS

1. To make the back of the caddie, measure and cut a 10 by 36-inch rectangle from the backing fabric. Hem the long sides and bottom of the backing. Fold the top down $^1/_2$ inch, toward the wrong side, and sew a casing. Press with the iron. Insert the eyelets evenly spaced across the top through the casing.

2. To make a pleated bottom pocket, measure and cut an 11 by 12-inch rectangle from the fabric for the large pocket. Stitch a $^1/_2$-inch hem at the top (a 12-inch side). Turn the side edges under $^1/_2$ inch, and press them with the iron. Press a 1-inch box pleat at each side. Topstitch (see resources section) this pocket onto the backing, positioned toward the bottom of the backing. For added strength, backstitch at the pocket top.

3. To make the medium-size pockets, measure and cut two 8 by 10-inch rectangles from the fabric. Trim the pockets with ribbon, iron-on letters, or rickrack as desired. Stitch $^1/_2$-inch hems in the tops, press the other edges under $^1/_2$ inch, and topstitch the pockets to the backing. For added strength, backstitch at the pocket tops.

4. Measure and cut as many small pockets as you'd like, in various sizes, from the fabric for those pockets, and stitch them to the backing as described in step 3.

5. To strengthen the caddie, use wire cutters to cut a 9-inch length of coat hanger wire from the straight part of a hanger, and insert it into the top casing of the backing.

6. To hang the caddie, thread the yarn or cord through the eyelets. Cut off the curved part of the top of the hanger and form a loop at the bottom with pliers. Tie the yarn through the bottom loop you just formed, hang your caddy in a handy spot, and fill it with everything you need.

HOLIDAY

FELT AND FOIL
Christmas Tree Ornaments

BE JOLLY
by golly!

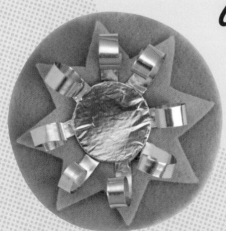

*I*nexpensive craft felt combined with items you have around the house, such as aluminum foil, foil pie pans, and tin can lids, become adorable and unique Christmas tree decorations.

MATERIALS

Heavy paper

Pencil

Holiday cards (if necessary)

Scissors

1 (15-inch-long) piece heavy-duty aluminum foil

Several layers of newspaper

Dull pencil

Colored nail polish for accent colors (optional)

Standard white craft glue (see page 6)

Yarn scraps

Sheets of (9 by 12-inch) craft felt in various colors (see page 4)

1 tin can lid

Can opener

Tin snips (see page 7)

1 aluminum foil pie pan

MAKES 4 FLAT FOIL ORNAMENTS AND 1 FRINGED-CENTER ORNAMENT

INSTRUCTIONS FOR FLAT FOIL ORNAMENTS

1. On heavy paper, draw holiday shapes such as angels, birds, and bells. If you need inspiration, look at the holiday cards, and trace the shapes onto the paper. Cut out the shapes.

2. Fold the foil in thirds as if you were folding a letter. Place the foil on the layers of newspaper. Lay a shape cutout on the foil, and trace around it, using the dull pencil (the pressure of the pencil helps hold the foil layers together). Cut out the foil shape. Repeat for the other shapes.

3. Paint designs and features on the foil with nail polish (see the angel and bell), or glue on yarn or felt trim (see the boot, butterfly, and bird in the vintage image).

4. Place your paper shapes on the felt pieces, and trace around them. Cut out shapes of felt, adding 1/4 inch all around the design. Glue the foil cutouts centered on the felt cutouts to create a colored outline effect.

INSTRUCTIONS FOR FRINGED-CENTER ORNAMENTS

1. The star and teardrop ornaments sandwich tin can lids between felt circles to give them stiffness. To begin, remove the lid from a tin can; either use a special can opener that leaves no sharp edges on the lid or use a regular can opener but be careful handling the lid.

2. Trace the lid twice onto felt pieces. Then cut out two felt circles or two teardrop shapes. Glue one to each side of the tin can lid.

3. To make silver-fringed centers, with tin snips, cut the rim from an aluminum foil pie pan (about $3/8$ inch down from the top edge). Snip partway through the cut edge every $1/4$ inch to make fringe. Curl the strip of fringe around a pencil. The rolled edge of the former pie pan rim becomes the base of the silver fringe.

4. Glue the base of the fringe to the felt ornament. If you like, paint some of the fringe with nail polish (see the red outer layer of fringe on the green circular ornament).

Holiday zip FOR *half* THE CLAMS!

Farm Journal Christmas Book copyright © 1948–1968 by Farm Journal, Inc.

FOIL SANTA

Yule flip for this shiny old **SAINT NICK!**

ere's a nifty way to gift-wrap a jar of cookies or candies for an extra-special holiday present. Once you've constructed the Santa, you can lift his body off the coffee can and place a jar of homemade cookies or candies in the can.

MATERIALS

1 empty coffee can

Aluminum foil

Ruler

Pencil

Red, white, and black construction paper

Scissors

Transparent tape (see page 7)

Standard white craft glue (see page 6)

1 (3-inch-diameter) Styrofoam ball

Loose pillow stuffing (see page 5)

1 disposable wooden chopstick

Red crepe paper or tissue paper

MAKES 1 SANTA JAR

INSTRUCTIONS

1. Place the coffee can right side up on top of a large piece of aluminum foil. Fold the foil smoothly up and over the sides of the can, crinkling it tightly inside the can to hold the foil in place.

2. Using the ruler and pencil, measure and mark a 7 by 12-inch rectangle on the red construction paper. Cut out the rectangle with the scissors, curve the paper into a cone shape, and fasten it with tape. Place the cone over the coffee can with the large end of the cone down to create Santa's body.

3. Form two long narrow cones (about 7 inches long and 4 inches in diameter) from the red construction paper. Fasten one cone on each side of the body by taping them to the top of the larger cone to form Santa's arms.

4. Cut two mitten shapes about $2^1/_2$ inches long from the white construction paper, and glue one to the inside of each cone arm.

5. To create Santa's foil belt, cut a strip of foil long enough to fit around Santa's waist and glue it to the body cone. Cut a rectangle of black construction paper for the belt buckle; cut a smaller rectangle from the center and glue the resulting buckle to the front of the foil belt. Crush some strips of foil around the ends of the arms to create foil cuffs.

6. Use the Styrofoam ball for the head. Cut face features from the black construction paper, and glue them to the ball. Glue on the pillow stuffing to make a beard. Stick the sharper end of the chopstick into the bottom of the Styrofoam ball. Spread some glue onto the top of the body cone and rest the Styrofoam ball on top, inserting the chopstick into the hole in the cone (the glue and chopstick will hold the head in place).

7. Form a narrow cone about 14 inches long from the red crepe paper or tissue paper, turn up the bottom to form a brim, then bend down the pointed end. Glue the hat to the top of the head.

8. Cut out two foot shapes about 3 inches long from the black construction paper. Glue them sticking out like feet to the underside of the coffee can.

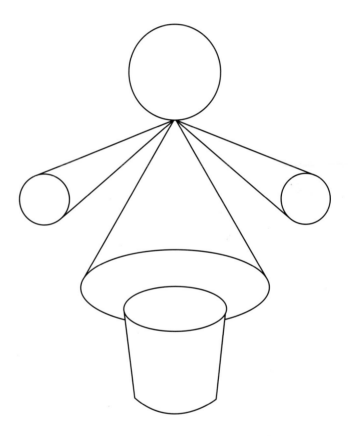

Lightbulb Christmas Ornaments

Here's a BRIGHT idea: Christmas tree ornaments made from burned-out lightbulbs!

*L*et your imagination run wild as you experiment with making ornaments from burned-out lightbulbs of different shapes and sizes. You can create an infinite variety of colorful Christmas tree decorations. (But can you even find burned-out lightbulbs with all these darned energy-efficient bulbs that last for years?)

MATERIALS

Burned-out lightbulbs in various shapes and sizes

Acrylic paint and paintbrush

Ribbon, yarn, or colorful cord (approximately 30 inches per bulb)

Standard white craft glue, or hot glue gun (see page 6 or 5)

Beads, sequins, and other decorations you like

MAKES 1 ORNAMENT PER BULB

INSTRUCTIONS

1. Paint the glass part of the bulb with the acrylic paint, and let it dry completely.

2. Wrap the ribbon, yarn, or cord tightly around the metal end of the lightbulb, and tie a bow or loop at the end.

3. Decorate the bulb by gluing the beads, sequins, or other embellishments to it. Hang your sparkly new decoration on the tree.

Glamorous PAPER Decorations

Beautiful holiday decorations use (or reuse) paper in clever, *thrifty ways!*

*U*se these pretty paper decorations in centerpieces, on gift wrappings, or as hanging ornaments on the tree or dangling from the ceiling. The color choices are up to you—use traditional green and red, or a subtle palette such as blue, green, turquoise, and gold. Using construction paper, gift wrap paper or sparkly metallic paper, you can create an infinite variety of ornaments from just the three basic patterns given here.

MATERIALS

Construction paper, gift wrap paper, or other decorative paper

Pair of compasses for drawing circles and curves

Pencil

Metal ruler

Protractor

Scissors

Metal nail file, or other dull-pointed instrument

Cardboard

Standard white craft glue (see page 6)

1 small round Christmas ornament, or bead, or marble (for the star)

Needle and thread

Transparent tape (see page 7)

MAKES 1 STAR, 1 CHINESE BALL, AND 1 LANTERN

INSTRUCTIONS FOR THE STAR

1. On the back side of your decorative paper, use the compasses to draw three circles, one inside another, 1 inch, 2 inches, and 4 inches in diameter (see diagram).

2. Divide each circle into 12 equal parts by using a ruler to draw lines through the center as shown in the diagram. Use the protractor to measure the angles for equal segments (or eyeball the measurements as carefully as possible). Draw the points of the star as shown, using straight and dotted lines. Cut out all the areas that are

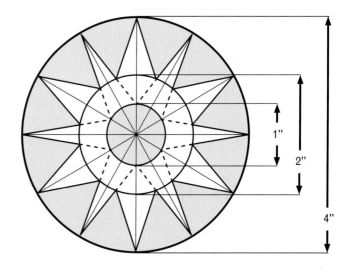

shaded in the diagram (leaving the star with a circle cut out of the middle).

3. Score all the straight lines with the nail file. Turn the paper right side up, and fold the scored lines toward you; working on the back side, fold the dotted lines away from the right side.

4. Cut out a circle of cardboard and a circle of construction paper 5 inches in diameter; glue the two together. Use craft glue to attach areas at the back of the star to the cardboard. Glue the small round Christmas ornament in the center of the front of the star.

5. To make larger stars, increase the diameters of the circles to 1¹/₂, 3, and 6 inches or 2, 4, and 8 inches.

6. To hang the ornament, poke a threaded needle through the cardboard about ¹/₄ inch from the edge and tie a loop with the thread.

INSTRUCTIONS FOR THE CHINESE BALL

1. Cut a 4 by 11-inch rectangle out of decorative paper. On the back side, draw a horizontal line 1¹/₄ inches from the top; draw a second horizontal line 1¹/₂ inches down from the first line (see diagram). Draw vertical lines 1 inch apart so you have eleven 1-inch sections.

2. Starting halfway over in the top quadrant, draw zigzag lines as shown (see diagram). Cut out the zigzags, and join the left and right ends together with the tape. With the needle and

CHINESE BALL PATTERN

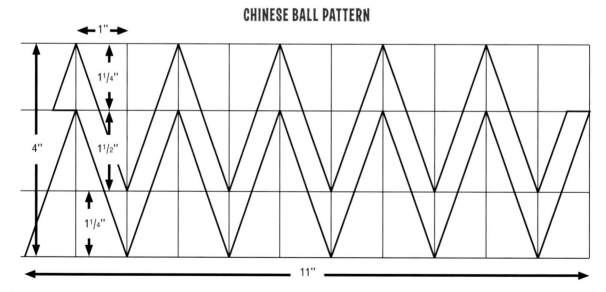

The Craftster Guide to Nifty, Thrifty, and Kitschy Crafts

thread, sew near the top points of the zigzags, pull the thread to bring the points together, and knot the thread to secure them. Repeat with the bottom points.

3. To make larger balls, increase the size of the rectangle to $5^1/_2$ by $14^1/_2$ inches, and draw the horizontal lines $1^3/_4$ inches from the top and bottom and 2 inches apart, but still divide into 11 equal parts with vertical lines. To make even larger balls, make the rectangle $9^1/_8$ by $18^1/_4$ inches, and draw the horizontal lines $2^7/_8$ inches from the top and bottom, but still make 11 equal parts across.

4. To hang the ornament, poke a threaded needle into the top of the ball about $^1/_4$ inch from the edge and tie a loop with the thread.

INSTRUCTIONS FOR THE LANTERN

1. Cut a 4 by $10^3/_4$-inch rectangle out of the decorative paper.

2. On a piece of cardboard, create a template for the rounded triangle shape shown in the diagram. The triangle is $1^5/_{16}$ inches wide at the base and $1^7/_8$ inches high.

3. Place the decorative paper right side down, and trace around your cardboard pattern seven times on one long edge (see diagram), leaving $^3/_{16}$ inch between the bases of adjacent triangles. Repeat the tracing on the other long edge of the paper. Add the dotted lines.

4. Score the dotted and solid lines with the metal nail file. Fold the dotted lines away from you

LANTERN PATTERN

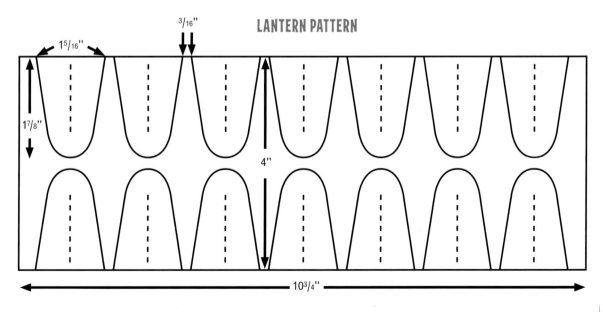

(toward the front of the decorative paper) and fold the solid lines toward you (away from the front of the paper). Glue the short ends of the paper together, decorative side out. With the needle and thread, gather the top edges together and tie a knot to secure them. Do the same with the bottom edges.

5. To make larger lanterns, increase the size of the rectangle of paper to $5^3/4$ by $11^1/8$ inches and the size of the rounded triangle to $1^3/8$ inches wide by $2^3/4$ inches high; or increase the rectangle to $8^1/2$ by $19^7/8$ inches and the triangle to $2^5/8$ inches wide by 4 inches high.

6. To hang the ornament, poke a threaded needle into the top of the lantern about $1/4$ inch from the edge and tie a loop with the thread.

SPACE-AGE *Party Accessories*

"*Blast Off*" with a space-themed party!

*N*o space party would be complete without a big shiny rocket. Making one—or a bunch—plus a huge (but lightweight) space helmet can be a blast. Disclaimer: The helmet depicted in this project will not protect you from those voices you sometimes hear in your head. The little would-be astronaut in your life will be thrilled to have a space helmet in his or her size for Halloween or another costume affair.

MATERIALS

1 large balloon (inflatable to 16 inches in diameter)

Aluminum foil

Scissors

Hot glue gun (see page 5)

Paper or plastic cups, or empty thread spools

1 or more sheets heavy paper (size and number depending on what size and how many rockets you want to make)

Transparent tape (see page 7)

Cardboard

MAKES 1 SPACE HELMET AND 1 OR MORE ROCKETS

INSTRUCTIONS FOR THE SPACE HELMET

1. Inflate the balloon to the desired size for the helmet (10 to 12 inches in diameter for children and 12 to 16 inches for adults), and knot it. Using several 3-foot-long pieces of foil, cover the balloon entirely.

2. At the bottom of the helmet, cut a hole for your head to fit through (popping the balloon in the process; remove the balloon). Then cut a semicircle out of the lower half of the helmet for the face opening. Use more sheets of foil to smooth over the raw edges that were created by cutting the holes.

3. Using the hot glue gun, attach the cups or spools (for knobs), and glue on antennae made from crushed foil.

INSTRUCTIONS FOR THE ROCKET

1. Roll a sheet of the heavy paper into a cylinder of whatever size you'd like the rocket to be. Use the tape to hold it together.

2. Cut a semicircle from the cardboard, and tape the corners together to make the nose cone. Cut fins from the cardboard, too. To attach these parts to the cylinder and simultaneously give the rocket a metallic sheen, cover everything with aluminum foil.

3. Repeat to make more rockets as tiny or huge (5 feet or more) as your materials allow.

FOLDED-MAGAZINE *Valentine Girl*

CHARM YOUR STEADY WITH THIS *clever valentine* MADE FROM OLD MAGAZINES.

IT SAYS MORE THAN WORDS *ever* COULD!

I have two vintage craft books by two different authors in my collection that are all about making figures out of small folded magazines. My theory is that some brilliant teacher learned that this kind of project could keep kids busy for hours, folding page after page. I recommend a small, thick magazine, such as *TV Guide* or *Reader's Digest*, for this project, because it makes a nice-size doll and has enough pages to form a sturdy base.

MATERIALS

1 small-format magazine

Stapler

Standard white craft glue (see page 6)

Measuring tape

Scissors

Square piece of cardboard (width and height should be twice the width of a page of the magazine)

White spray paint (see page 6) and newspapers, or white acrylic paint (see page 3) and paintbrush

1 cone-shaped piece of Styrofoam at least 4 inches long

Craft knife (see page 3)

2 white chenille stems (see page 3)

1 (3-inch-diameter) Styrofoam ball

12 cotton balls, or loose pillow stuffing (see page 5)

1/2 yard (1/4-inch-wide) red satin ribbon

1 bunch small artificial flowers

1/4 yard (2 1/2-inch-wide) fringe

Construction paper scraps (including red, pink, and black) for eyes, mouth, and valentine heart

Sequins for the valentine (optional)

MAKES 1 VALENTINE GIRL

INSTRUCTIONS

1. Open the magazine to the first page and gently fold (do not crease sharply) the top outer corners of the two facing pages diagonally down toward the center. Staple each page at the folded-over corner (see figure 1). Turn to the next facing pages, and repeat the folding and stapling until you've gently folded about 200 pages (100 sets of two). Carefully tear off the rest of the magazine (a page or two at a time so you don't destroy the binding of the magazine).

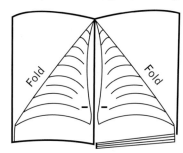

2. Open up the folded pages so that they fall into a complete circle (this will be the skirt of the doll). Glue the first page to the last page, so the skirt stands up on its own. To space the folds evenly around the skirt and add strength to the doll, measure the circumference of the skirt at the bottom, and cut a circle of the cardboard that size. Glue the skirt bottom to the cardboard to make a base.

3. Spray- or hand-paint the skirt "pages" white, and allow them to dry completely. (If you use spray paint, first spread out protective newspaper to catch the excess, and paint outdoors or in a well-ventilated room.)

4. Measure 4 inches from the tip of the Styrofoam cone. Using the craft knife, trim away the excess Styrofoam from the widest end so you have a 4-inch-tall cone. Turned upside down, the cone creates the doll's body. To attach the cone to the skirt, cut a 6-inch piece of chenille stem, and stick one end into the bottom of the body (the narrowest side) and the other end into the hole at the top of the skirt. Attach the Styrofoam ball to the top of the body similarly with a small piece of chenille stem; this creates the doll's head.

2¹/₂"

2¹/₂"

1"

5. Cut two more 6-inch pieces of chenille stem for the arms, and stick them into either side of the body. Bend the arms forward so they meet in front as if the doll were clasping her hands together.

6. To decorate the doll, glue puffs of the cotton balls to the head to create hair. Tie the satin ribbon into a bow around the doll's head. Use another piece of the ribbon to make a bow for the doll's skirt. Glue the bow to the back of the

skirt and glue flowers on the skirt in whatever pattern you desire. Glue a piece of fringe around the top of the body to create a lacy shawl. Cut a heart-shaped valentine out of construction paper, decorate it with sequins if you wish, and glue it to the doll's hands as if she were holding it. Make a pair of eyes and a mouth from the construction paper, and glue them to the doll's face.

Projects Made of Folded Magazines copyright © 1966 by Aleene's, Inc.

DOLL CAKE

WHAT A **LUSCIOUS, BEAUTIFUL** DOLL!

*T*he doll cake was once a staple of little girls' birthday parties. The dome shape of the cake becomes the doll's skirt. You can use a plastic doll or a "doll pick"—a special doll made for cakes that has a pick rather than legs, to set atop your cake. Some cake pans, such as the Wilton Wonder Mold, come in perfect dome shapes. If you can't find a dome-shaped pan, use an oven-safe metal or glass mixing bowl.

MATERIALS

Dome-shaped cake pan

Doll or doll pick

Sheet cake pan at least as wide and long as the dome pan's diameter (optional)

Mixer and mixing bowl

2 boxes cake mix (flavor of your choice)

Ingredients required by the cake mix directions

Cake plate

Long-bladed knife (if using a doll, not a doll pick)

Plastic wrap or aluminum foil (if using a doll)

Frosting spatula

2 tubs white frosting or 2 boxes white frosting mix

Food coloring for frosting (colors of your choice)

Frosting decoration bag and tips in various shapes (available at kitchen supply stores, supermarkets, or craft supply stores)

MAKES 1 CAKE

A cake's party dress is its Frosting

INSTRUCTIONS

1. To make sure that the cake pan you are using will create a deep enough skirt to cover the doll or doll pick from the waist down, turn the dome-shaped pan upside down, and stand the doll next to it. The height of the pan should come higher than the doll's waist. If it's lower, you can also bake a flat sheet cake the needed inches high, cut a circle out of it as wide as the dome pan, and then add it as a bottom layer under the dome-shaped cake.

2. Mix and bake the cake according to the directions on the box. Allow the cake to cool completely; then place it flat side down on a cake plate.

3. If you are using a doll rather than a doll pick, use a knife to hollow out a narrow hole in the center of the dome cake. Cover the doll's legs in plastic wrap or aluminum foil, and insert the doll into the center of the cake. If you're using a doll pick, just stick it into the center of the cake.

4. Using a frosting spatula, frost the entire cake with one thin, even layer of frosting. Then color the remaining frosting, pack it into the decoration bag, and have fun creating a bodice and ruffles or flowers all over the skirt with the decoration tips.

Resource Guide

VINTAGE FABRICS

www.makemefabrics.com

Carries an interesting variety of vintage fabrics and vintage buttons, buckles, pom-pom fringe, and other notions. Some new fabrics and a fun selection of fake fur.

www.revivalfabrics.com

Offers vintage fabric for quilting, making clothes, and home decorating. Carefully categorized by era and style.

VINTAGE-REPRODUCTION AND RETRO-THEMED FABRICS

www.contemporarycloth.com

Has a great selection of retro-inspired fabrics along with some actual vintage fabrics.

www.equilter.com

Offers an absolutely enormous selection of cotton prints, including many retro-themed prints. Broken down by category so you can easily find what you want.

www.reprodepot.com

Specializes in new cotton prints that have a retro vibe. Broken down into decades like Roaring Twenties and Fabulous Fifties. An excellent place to find things like atomic bark cloth, when actual vintage bark cloth is too expensive for your project.

VINTAGE CRAFT PATTERNS

www.abebooks.com

Provides a huge network of used-book dealers offering every kind of book under the sun. A great place to find vintage craft books—especially if you know the title or publisher.

www.colonialpatterns.com

Carries a selection of new reproductions of classic embroidery patterns, such as Aunt Martha's "days of the week" tea towel patterns.

www.rustyzipper.com

Specializes in vintage clothing but also has a good selection of original vintage patterns and craft books.

www.sublimestitching.com

Features hip new embroidery patterns with a retro sensibility.

www.vintage-knitting-patterns.com

Makes available carefully reproduced copies of vintage knitting patterns from 1915 to 1963 to download or on CD.

CRAFT SUPPLIES FOR RETRO CRAFT PROJECTS

The following online stores sell a variety of supplies on the kitschier side of things, such as plastic beads, pom-poms, small plastic favors and miniatures, doll faces, and potholder loops:

www.artcove.com
www.bjcraftsupplies.com
www.sunshinecrafts.com
www.craftking.com

ANYTHING AND EVERYTHING VINTAGE

At the following online auction sites you'll find people selling various lengths and styles of vintage fabric, vintage curtains and sheets to make things out of, vintage sewing notions, and old craft books and craft patterns:

www.ebay.com
www.rubylane.com
www.tias.com

CRAFTING RESOURCES

www.craftster.org

A community of craft lovers sharing all kinds of hip project ideas for every kind of craft. Retro-themed crafts are often popular here.

www.knitty.com

An informative resource for knitting with a hip sensibility.

www.thistothat.com

A fabulous resource whenever you need to know what kind of glue to use for a project. Just enter the two materials you're gluing together, and this site tells you the right kind of glue.

www.stitchguide.com

A comprehensive guide to any kind of stitch you need to know how to do for a variety of needlework techniques, including sewing, knitting, crocheting, and embroidery.

www.sewing.about.com

Sewing definitions, how-to articles, and many links to other good sewing websites.

About the Author

LEAH KRAMER has been a self-proclaimed craft junkie since she could hold a pair of safety scissors. In her spare time, Leah combs the aisles of thrift stores, yard sales, and flea markets looking for items to add to her collection of everything weird, old, and eye-catching, including 1950s craft and cookbooks, kitschy plastic charms, cake decorations, and old records with beautiful covers. Combining her computer skills with her love of crafting, Leah started the popular web community Craftster.org, whose motto is "No Tea Cozies without Irony," in 2003. Much to her surprise, the website is now visited by hundreds of thousands of like-minded crafters. Part-owner of the Somerville, Massachusetts, boutique called Magpie, which sells hip crafts and goods by indie designers and artists, Leah is also an organizer of the popular punk rock craft fair, Bazaar Bizarre (bazaarbizarre.org). Leah lives and crafts in Boston, Massachusetts.